CRE Glossary of Terms

CRE Glossary of Terms – 1st Edition

Published by: www.adventuresincre.com, LLC
www.AdventuresinCRE.com

Copyright © 2022 by www.adventuresincre.com, LLC
All rights reserved. No portion of this book may be reproduced in any form without permission from the publisher, except as permitted by U.S. copyright law. For permissions contact: admin@adventuresincre.com

Cover and book design by Nela Nikolovska and Ana Secivanovic

ISBN: 979-8-9868731-0-7
Printed in United States of America
1st Edition

The online resource for commercial real estate professionals worldwide, including real estate financial models and training, career advice, CRE education insights, and networking opportunities.

1031 Exchange

A common real estate practice with origins in the IRS code section 1031, which allows investors to essentially swap one property for another in an effort to defer capital gains taxes. The two properties must be "like-kind" properties and used in a trade or business as an investment. 1031 exchanges must meet multiple other requirements. If executed successfully, however, investors can save large amounts via deferred capital gains taxes, which helps spur ongoing investment.

Absorption

See net absorption and gross absorption.

A.CRE

An acronym for the website www.adventuresincre.com, pronounced "A-C-R-E."

Acre

A unit of land that equals 43,560 square feet, or 4046.85642 square meters.

Acuity Spectrum

A range of care which encompasses the categories within senior living. The continuum typically ranges (in order of increasing acuity) from independent living to assisted living to memory care to nursing care.

Adaptive Reuse

A repositioning strategy in real estate whereby the investor converts the use and/or design of an existing building into something new. Typical scenarios include the conversion of industrial building, schools and churches into other building types such as residences, museums or art galleries.

Add Alternate

An additional item of work that is priced out by a consultant/subcontractor during the contract negotiation or bid process, but which is not yet part of the scope of work. It is an item that an owner is considering adding to the consultant's/subcontractor's contract, but which has not yet been confirmed as to whether the service is wanted. As a result, the owner would like to know/negotiate the price for this item in the case they decide to move forward with it post contract agreement.

Example: The owner of a multifamily residential project is hiring an interior designer to do the layouts for five different floor plans. The owner is also considering having the interior designer do the penthouse as well. Although not currently part of the scope, the owner wants to know/negotiate the price for designing the penthouse and requests the interior designer to include an add alternate for designing the penthouse in case they decide to pursue the option.

Adjusted Funds from Operations

A superior metric compared to FFO when evaluating a REIT's performance. AFFO is used in order to account for any additional expenses the landlord is expected to incur over the life of the asset (such as TIs, CAPEX, leasing commissions etc.). The measure is calculated as follows:

AFFO = FFO − Maintenance Costs − CAPEX − Straight Line Rent Adjustments.

Adjusted Funds from Operations is comparable to the cash flow from operations line item used in analyzing individual properties.

ADR

See Average Daily Rate.

Adverse Possession

Also referred to as Squatter's Rights, adverse possession enables a person living on or using someone else's property to legally take ownership of said property if the original owner has abandoned and/or not claimed ownership over a certain period of time. This law came into effect to encourage land/property upkeep and utilization. Adverse Possession can be determined by the mnemonic *HELUVA: Hostile, Exclusive, Lasting, Uninterrupted, Visible, Actual*. A squatter must demonstrate the following actions in order to legally take ownership of a property:

Hostile - possess property with no permission from original owner

Exclusive - be the only person/family to possess the property and keep it exclusive from others

Lasting - lasts for the statutory period as set by states

Uninterrupted - continuous possession

Visible - open and notorious about possession

Actual - must actually possess the land and inhabit as intended

Affidavit of Title

See Owner's Affidavit.

Affirmative Covenant

A type of restrictive property covenant that obligates the landowner to act. This covenant runs with the land, meaning that even in transfer of ownership, the obligation remains with the new landowner. An example of an affirmative covenant may be an obligation for the landowner to maintain a certain level and type of insurance or to maintain the property at a certain standard.

AFFO

See Adjusted Funds from Operations.

Age-restricted Community

In commercial real estate, this typically refers to a restriction on residential communities, where residents must be a certain age or older, often 55+. Investors often see these communities to have an advantage based on residents having surpassed periods in life with conflict (such as divorce or income difficulties), where residents may have also downsized from traditional housing and have more steady income (either from fixed pensions or social security payments) than demographics of all-age communities.

American-style Waterfall

A common method for distributing investment cash flow between two or more partners. An American-Style waterfall refers to a form of equity waterfall where the sponsor (i.e., general partner) is eligible to receive a promote (i.e., carried interest) before the limited partner has received a full return of capital and earned a preferred return. As such, distributable cash flow during operations and distributable cash flow at a capital event are treated differently.

While referred to as American-style, this form of real estate partnership waterfall is common worldwide, including in Europe. It is often preferred by general partners as it front loads distributions to the general partner.

Architect

In commercial real estate, architects are typically present throughout the entire development process through design and construction and different architects may serve in different functions on the same project such as design architect and architect of record. Architects lead the design process and typically oversee the construction of a building on behalf of the ownership and to ensure the project is being built as intended in the design.

Architect of Record

The architect of record is the architect or firm that creates the construction documents for a new project. The architect of record's name will also appear on the building permit issued for that specific building project.

Assignee

An entity that receives the rights to a property from an assignor. A mortgagee is an example of an assignee.

Assignor

An entity that transfers the right it has to a property to a third party. A mortgagor is an example of an assignor.

Average Daily Rate

The average revenue generated per paid occupied room per day, calculated by dividing total room revenue by the number of rooms sold. The ADR is commonly used in the hospitality industry together with the RevPAR metric to assess the property's performance.

Average Life

Also referred to as Weighted Average Life, or WAL, the average life of a mortgage loan refers to the number of periods (commonly denoted in years) in which half the time-weighted principal has been paid. Lenders use this metric in a variety of ways, including to price the loan (i.e., as part of the benchmark calculation to arrive at an appropriate interest rate) and to compare the risk of two loans of similar loan maturity.

Average Rate of Return

A measure of the profitability of a real estate investment and a type of return metric. The average rate of return is calculated as the total net profit of an investment (total cash inflows minus total cash outflows), divided by the length of the investment, divided by the invested capital. The main drawback of this return metric is that it does not take into account the time value of money.

Average Rate of Return = Total Net Profit ÷ Investment Period ÷ Equity Contributed

Example: An investor purchases a retail center for $1,000 all cash. The investor holds the center for 10 years during which time the investment earns $100 each year. At the end of the 10-year period, the investor sells the property for $1,500. The average rate of return of this investment is:

15% = 1,500 ÷ 10 years ÷ 1,000

Axonometric

An architectural drawing that depicts an object in three dimensions. This is commonly created by architects to show others a more realistic depiction of a current project.

Bad Boy Carveouts

See Non-Recourse Carveouts.

Balance Sheet Investing

When an investor uses its own funds to invest in a real estate asset. This is in contrast to using 3rd party funds (when referring to equity) or securitization proceeds (when referring to debt).

Balloon Payment

The final payment on a loan. In commercial real estate, the balloon payment is the entire outstanding balance of the loan as of the loan maturity date. A balloon payment is only due when the loan has not been fully amortized.

For instance, a lender extends a mortgage loan of $10,000,000, for a term of five years, with interest-only payments for the entire five years. The balloon payment at loan maturity will be $10,000,000.

In another example, a lender extends a mortgage loan of $10,000,000, for a term of 10 years, with payments amortized over 30 years. While the loan is amortizing, it will not be fully amortized at loan maturity (year 10) and thus the borrower will owe a balloon payment for the balance due.

When underwriting a perspective loan, real estate lenders take special care to analyze the likelihood the borrower will be able to pay off the balloon payment at maturity. They use tools such as refinance analysis risk models to assess whether a payoff of the balloon balance is likely.

Bargain and Sale Deed

A bargain and sale deed only guarantees that the grantor has title to the property and the right to transfer ownership but does not guarantee that it is free of encumbrances. It also doesn't guarantee that the title is free of any defects.

It is not uncommon for bargain and sale deeds to come with or without covenants.

Base Year Stop

Upon lease commencement, the building owner will agree to pay the tenant's first year expenses (a.k.a. base year expenses) and will continue to pay the same amount in each of the subsequent years while the tenant will pay any additional costs above the amount realized in the base year. So, in a base year stop scenario, the building owner's costs for op ex is capped to the amount the he or she had to pay in year 1. So, if year 1 expenses were $1k, and year 2 expenses were $1.5k, then the landlord would still pay $1k in year 2 and the tenants would pay $500 difference.

Bid and Award Process

The period during which the owner and/or general contractor solicit bids from numerous subcontractors (subs) from the trades needed to build a project. Once the subs have responded to the bid requests, the general contractor may request additional information or conduct interviews and subsequently awards a contract to the selected group for each needed trade. High quality construction documents are crucial at this stage in order to ensure subcontractors are able to accurately take off material estimates and make realistic project bids.

BOMA

See Building Owners and Managers Association.

Breakeven Occupancy

The occupancy at which the effective gross income is equal to the sum of the operating expenses plus debt service. Breakeven occupancy is an important metric for lenders, developers, and operators as it is the point at which the property shifts from an operating deficit to an operating surplus. Real estate owners will often use rent concessions to speed the investment to breakeven.

Point at which EGI = OpEx + DS; also, the point at which DSCR = 1.00

Example: A property has a potential gross income of $1,000 with $500 in operating expenses and $250 in debt service. Breakeven occupancy in this case would be calculated as (500 + 250) ÷ 1,000 = 75%.

Breakup Fee

A fee paid to one party in a real estate transaction by a counterparty when the counterparty backs out of the transaction. The breakup fee is generally a percentage of the purchase price or mortgage loan amount and is used to compensate the damaged party for time and resources spent on the transaction.

Bridge Loan

Also referred to as a mini-perm, in real estate a bridge loan is a short-term loan typically provided to developers and value-add real estate investors. This loan is used to "bridge" periods during which the property is not eligible for permanent financing. The term of a bridge loan can be anywhere from a few months to several years, and generally carries a higher interest rate commensurate with the higher risk to the lender.

Building Core

A main concrete structural component that goes the entire vertical length of a high-rise building and houses elevators, stairwells, and MEP vertical risers. In many cases, the core will also house the bathrooms in non-residential commercial buildings. Also see Core - (structural).

Building Owners and Managers Association

Founded in 1907, the Building Owners and Managers Association (BOMA) is an international real estate trade organization representing owners and managers of commercial real estate. The organization promotes, provides advocacy and develops various pertinent research publications in support of its members. BOMA members span the entire property and investment type spectrum. BOMA International is widely recognized as a primary source of information on building management and operations, development, leasing, building operating costs, energy consumption patterns, local and national building codes, legislation, occupancy statistics, technological developments and other industry trends.

Most notably, BOMA is the go-to resource that industry professionals work with to calculate accurate building measurements.

Buildup Rate

An alternative method for arriving at a capitalization rate for a real estate investment. The buildup rate is the sum of all risks of an investment (denoted in percentage) plus the risk-free interest rate.

For example:

Risk-Free Rate (e.g. 10-yr UST): 2.25%
+
Illiquid nature of investment: 0.75%
+
Credit risk of tenants: 1.25%
+
Inflation risk: 1.00%
+
And so forth...
=
Buildup rate: 5.25%

CAM
See Common Area Maintenance.

Cap Ex
See Capital Expenditure.

Cap Rate
The Cap Rate, or Capitalization Rate, is the percentage derived from a stabilized asset's annual NOI divided by its purchase price.

Cap Rate = Stabilized Annual NOI ÷ Asset Value

Investors often look to cap rates that have been set in the market to begin getting a ball park idea of what they might pay for an asset they are looking to invest in. For example, an investor is looking at a Class A office asset in X market. Class A office buildings in X market have been trading between a 5% - 6% cap rate over the past 6 months, so an investor may look to his or her first year of projected NOI and divide that by a cap rate of somewhere between 5% - 6% to get an idea of the price he or she might need to pay.

Capital Expenditure
In real estate, an expenditure with a useful life greater than one year. Referred to colloquially as CapEx, Capital Expenditures are depreciated over their useful life (e.g., $100,000 expenditure with 10-year useful life = $10,000 depreciation each year for 10 years). In contrast, operating

expenses are fully depreciated in the year they occur. In real estate modeling, capital expenditures fall below net operating income due to their volatile (sporadic) nature.

Carried Interest
See Promote.

Car Stacker
A hydraulic machine used to vertically stack cars in order to maximize parking efficiency. This technology is increasingly being used in high-density urban areas where land costs and parking rates make implementing this economically feasible.

Cash Sweep
The use of any free cash flow (after deducting debt service payments) to pay down an outstanding loan balance. In real estate, a cash sweep is often implemented by a lender when a borrower is unable to pay off the balloon balance upon loan maturity.

Cash-on-Cash Return
Before tax cash flow (BTCF = CFO - Debt Service) divided by the total equity contribution to date, expressed on an annual basis as a percentage.

Cash-on-Cash Return = Before Tax Cash Flow ÷ Total Equity Contribution to Date

The Cash-on-Cash Return of an investment is important when looking at stabilized cash flow on an annual basis.

The Cash-on-Cash Return is typically used alongside other return metrics such as the Equity Multiple, Internal Rate of Return, and Free and Clear Return to appropriately assess an investment.

Cash-out Refinance

The process by which a borrower takes out a new mortgage with sufficient loan proceeds to pay off the existing mortgage plus return all or part of the borrower's invested capital in the investment. The cash-out refinance is sought by owners of real estate because it provides them an opportunity to reduce their risk in the property while simultaneously freeing up capital to invest in new opportunities.

Catch-up Provision

A provision included in certain real estate partnership agreements, whereby a special distribution tier is included in the equity waterfall that allows for the general partner (GP) to "catch up" with the limited partner's (LP) cash flow distributions. The reason for why the general partner's distributions might lag, or the amount that must be made up with the "catch up" tier, depends on the terms of the partnership structure.

Catch up provisions are most common to structures where the limited partner receives 100% of distributions until it achieves some preferred return requirement, at which point the GP receives 100% of excess cash flow thereafter until some equitable balance between the LP and GP distributions is achieved.

For example, imagine a limited partner contributes 100% of required capital to a real estate venture in return for a 12% preferred return and 50% of all excess cash flows above that threshold. The agreement states that the limited partner will receive 100% of all cash distributions until it has earned a 12% internal rate of return, at which point the GP receives 100% of cash distributions until both partners have received 50% of profit distributions. Once the GP has caught up with the LP, both partners receive any remaining excess cash flow at a 50/50 split.

Central Business District

The central business district (CBD) is typically the center of business and economic activity of a city. Land use is generally more dense urban infill with various land uses, including retail, office, hotel, government, and entertainment buildings, as well as higher density housing.

CBD

See Central Business District.

CCIM

See Certified Commercial Investment Member.

CCIP

See Contractor Controlled Insurance Program.

CCRC
See Continuing Care Retirement Community.

Certified Commercial Investment Member

A commercial real estate designation issued by the CCIM Institute. The abbreviation CCIM stands for Certified Commercial Investment Member.

To earn the CCIM designation, candidates must complete an education component, demonstrate experience in commercial real estate, and sit for a comprehensive exam. The CCIM designation generally takes 1-3 years to complete.

Civil Engineer

Civil engineers are responsible for supervising the design and construction of multiple types of infrastructure, including roads, sewage treatment systems, bridges, waterways and multiple other projects. Civil engineers must ensure that a project adheres to all applicable construction laws, environmental regulations, or any other applicable statutes.

Clawback Provision

A provision included in certain real estate partnership agreements, whereby a special distribution tier is included in the equity waterfall that allows for the limited partner (LP) to "clawback" cash flow previously distributed to the general partner (GP).

Reasons for including the clawback provision vary but are generally related to instances where the GP is distributed cash flow before the LP reaches a preferred return hurdle. In the event at the end of the venture where the LP has not achieved some preferred return, the GP must give back some or all distributions previously made to the GP until such point that the LP hits its preferred return.

Cold Shell
Any building/rentable area that consists only of a bare, unimproved shell, i.e., no interior finishes, HVAC, plumbing, lighting, elevators etc.

Common Area Maintenance
Common Area Maintenance, commonly referred to as CAM, is a term used in commercial real estate leases that is meant to address the cost of building operations that all tenants benefit from and will pay for. Tenants usually pay a portion of CAM as determined by the negotiated agreement, but often times it is the tenant's pro rata share. Elements of CAM costs vary, but common CAM items may include janitorial services, landscaping, common area electricity, security, trash removal, and snow removal.

Community Center ("Large Neighborhood Center")
A community center is a retail subtype distinguished for its convenience-oriented offerings and general merchandise,

wide range of clothing stores, and a higher variety of goods than Neighborhood Centers. Off-price retailers, supermarkets, and large-specialty discount stores are common types of anchor tenants for this retail subtype. The trade area is approximately 3 to 6 miles, with centers averaging around 200,000 SF or larger.

Source: ICSC

Conceptual Design

A pre-design phase where the owner and architectural and environmental team work together to bring shape to the project and outline its function and form. The conceptual design promotes an open dialogue between the architect and the owner, with concept sketches often being used to illustrate and communicate ideas and expectations.

Concessions

Also referred to as an "inducement," any preferential financial treatment offered by one party to another in a real estate transaction. In the case of a lease agreement, a concession most often takes the form of free rent for a period of time or an agreement by the landlord to waive certain charges such as parking charges or pet fees. These concessions are meant to induce the tenant to sign the lease. Concessions are most often used during initial lease-up (i.e., when a building first delivers) or during tenant-friendly periods in the market cycle to maintain rent rates.

Construction Documents

Detailed documents of the development project put together by the A&E team after the Design Development Phase of the design process. The Construction Documents (CDs) reflect the finalized building design and provide specific details to communicate to the contractor and subcontractors how the project should be constructed. These legally binding documents are used during construction by all the trades and are also initially used to obtain bids from contractors and subcontractors. CDs, at minimum, will include numerous detailed drawings of the project and a specifications manual.

Construction Financing

A short-term loan, typically with a floating interest rate, issued by a lender to finance the construction of a real estate project. The loan is paid out to the borrower in draws as construction progresses. After construction is complete and the property is fully leased and/or sold, the loan is repaid using permanent loan proceeds or proceeds from the sale of the property.

Construction-Perm Loan

Also referred to as a "Rollover Loan," a construction-perm loan is a loan that starts off as a construction loan and immediately converts into permanent debt financing once construction of the project is finalized and the property is stabilized.

Construction to Permanent Loan

See Construction-Perm Loan.

Contingency Cost

An estimated amount of money added to a construction budget set aside by the developer and/or the contractor in order to account for any unknown risks (added and unexpected costs) associated with the project. These costs are designed to cover unforeseen expenses which are not precisely known at the time of estimate but which the contractor expects will occur based on statistical probabilities and personal experience.

Continuing Care Retirement Community

A senior living community that caters to a broad category of needs including independent and assisted living, as well as permanent skilled nursing care. CCRC's (also known as "life plan" communities) typically have high occupancy levels as they provide residents with the ability to "age in place."

Contract Rent

See also In-Place Rent. Contract Rent is the rent being charged and collected on existing leases at a property. In contrast to Market Rent, contract rent is not based on market conditions but rather is based on the lease contract signed between the landlord and tenant.

Contractor Controlled Insurance Program

OCIP (Owner Controlled Insurance Program) and CCIP (Contractor Controlled Insurance Program) are broad and all-encompassing insurance policies that usually cover, at a minimum, general liability insurance, worker's compensation, and excess liability insurance for all contractors and subcontractors on a construction project. An OCIP is sponsored and held by the owner, in contrast to a CCIP, which is sponsored and held by the contractor. The sponsor holds and is directly responsible for securing the appropriate and required insurance coverage.

Convenience or Strip Center

This retail subtype is characterized by having a row of stores, with on-site parking often found in the front of the stores. Open canopies may be used to connect store fronts of the tenants at the center. Average size may be 10,000 - 15,000 SF and larger, with a trade area of less than 1 mile. A typical anchor for these types of centers may be convenience stores, such as a mini mart.

Source: ICSC

Core

See Core - (investment strategy) or Core - (structural).

Core - (investment strategy)

A real estate investment strategy categorized by low risk

and commensurately low, stable returns. Core investment strategies typically involve longer hold periods, lower levels of leverage, and higher quality assets. Core investments are generally stabilized properties with high occupancy rates and predictable cash flows. Investors of core real estate investments value stable, reliable and consistent cash flows over price appreciation.

Core - (structural)

A vertical space in a multi-story building that commonly houses the elevators, stairwells, space for vertical MEP distribution, janitorial closets, and restrooms. It is common for buildings to have the core space in the center of the building, but the design and development team may sometimes elect to create a side core for various reasons such as if a central core would create inefficient floor plates that would not compete with the market.

Core Plus

Core Plus assets are properties that are otherwise Core assets (see Core - (investment strategy)), but with some component of risk (opportunity) attached to it. It may be a high street retail building with a tenant that takes 10% - 15% of the space vacating in 2 years and the space needs to be upgraded and re-leased. Or it could be an otherwise Core office tower located a bit outside of the prime office submarket with a lease or two that is a bit below market. A levered IRR for this risk profile could be between around 8% to 13%.

The four CRE Risk Profiles:
- *Core*
- *Core Plus*
- *Value Add*
- *Opportunistic*

Cost Plus Contract

A contract whereby the contractor is reimbursed for all the construction related costs, in addition to an agreed upon percentage of such costs covering the contractor's overhead and profit. These contracts are typically used when the scope of works is unclear, however they require additional owner supervision (in comparison to Fixed Price Contracts) as the contractor is less incentivized to exercise prudent cost controls.

Co-tenancy Clause

Co-tenancy clauses appear in retail leases and generally grant the tenant reduced rent, lease termination rights, or other privileges if other tenants, typically anchor tenants, vacate in the shared retail center (e.g., a shopping mall or grocery-anchored retail center). These clauses offer some protection to the tenant if another major tenant that is the primary draw for traffic to the center vacates.

CPI Rent Escalation

A form of contractual rent increase determined by changes in the Consumer Price Index (CPI), a common index used to measure inflation in the United States. Most long-term leases in commercial real estate include periodic rent increases. These rent increases are included in leases, in part, to ensure that the value of the lease does not diminish over time due to inflation.

Generally, the amount or percentage of the increase is pre-defined (e.g., $2/SF/YR, 2.5%/year, 10% every five years, etc.). However, in some cases the landlord and tenant agree to use the change in the Consumer Price Index to determine the periodic increase.

So if, for instance, the lease calls for annual CPI rent escalations, the rent due to the landlord will increase each year by the amount that CPI increases each year.

Note that while the Consumer Price Index is administered by the U.S. Bureau of Labor Statistics and in real estate is most commonly seen in US-based leases, it is not uncommon to also see CPI rent escalations in non-US leases when those leases are denominated in US Dollars (e.g. USD-denominated Industrial Leases in Mexico).

Cross-docked

In an industrial cross-docked building, dock doors are located on opposite sides of the building (typically the front and rear), which allows for the unloading of goods from inbound delivery trucks and loading the same goods directly onto outbound trucks. Typically, there is little to no storage between the dock doors to inhibit the process.

Crystallization

Also referred to as a partnership crystallization, a crystallization is a provision in a real estate joint venture agreement where the partners agree to adjust the ownership share in the venture at some pre-defined point in the future. It is most common to value-add and opportunistic investments, where a large increase in value is likely to be realized early in the investment.

The purpose of the crystallization is to allow the GP to earn its promote by way of a resetting of the ownership share percentages. The concept goes something like this:

At a point in time when the crystallization is to occur, the partners run the proceeds of a hypothetical sale through the equity waterfall to calculate the expected distribution to each partner. Based on that expected distribution, the ownership share is adjusted to reflect the share of the distribution each partner would hypothetically receive.

So for instance, imagine a JV where the GP owns 10% and the LP 90%. At crystallization, the partners assume a $100 million sale and run those proceeds through the waterfall model. The model calculates that, based on the promote structure and terms of the JV agreement, the GP would be distributed $17 million at sale and the LP would be distributed $83 million at sale.

The ownership share (i.e. the percentage distributed to each partner) from that moment forward would be 17% to the GP and 83% to the LP. And no further promote would be paid to the GP (the promote would be frozen).

Curtailment

A type of prepayment which reduces a mortgage loan's outstanding principal balance. Curtailment can be done by either increasing one's monthly payments or repaying a lump sum amount, both of which would shorten the loan maturity period.

Dark Value

The dark value is often analyzed by lenders to more completely understand risk. It refers to the value of the property should the main tenant "go dark" or vacate the property. This is a more crucial risk metric in scenarios where there is a single tenant in the building.

DCF

See Discounted Cash Flow.

Debt Covenants

Debt covenants are essentially rules written into the loan documents which govern the behavior of a borrower once the debt is issued. There are 2 general types of covenants which either permit (affirmative covenant) or restrict (negative covenant) the borrower's ability to perform certain actions. Should the borrower break a covenant, the lender typically has the legal right to call back the loan (i.e., demand repayment).

Debt Service Coverage Ratio

A financial metric used in real estate to measure a property's ability to cover its debt obligations. The Debt Service Coverage Ratio (DSCR or DSC) is calculated by dividing the net operating income by the debt service payment and is often expressed as a multiple (i.e., a DSCR of 1.20x). The DSCR is used by banks to determine the maximum loan amount offered to a borrower and to assess the probability that a borrower might default on the loan.

Debt Yield

The ratio of Net Operating Income (NOI) to the mortgage loan amount, expressed as a percentage. The debt yield is useful to lenders as it represents the lender's return on cost were it to take ownership of the property. Among other metrics, lenders use debt yield to determine an appropriate loan amount.

Debtor

See Mortgagor.

Deed

A legal written document that transfers possession of real property from one entity to another. Deeds are recorded at time of sale and when purchasing real estate. It is important to have a title search done where, among other things, a title company will review all the public records to see the chain of title, meaning they will review all the previous deeds recorded in connection with a property and if there were any breaks or gaps.

Common types of deeds: General Warranty Deed, Special Warranty Deed (Limited Warranty Deed), Quitclaim Deed, Bargain and Sale Deed, Grant Deed

Deed in Lieu of Foreclosure

The voluntary transfer of a title deed by the borrower to the lender in order to satisfy a defaulting loan (thereby avoiding foreclosure proceedings). Also referred to as "giving back the keys" or "jingle mail."

Deed of Trust

A Deed of Trust is an agreement between a lender (mortgagee) and borrower (mortgagor) whereby the mortgaged property is conveyed to a third neutral party (trustee), usually a title company, to be used as collateral while there is an outstanding mortgage. The mortgagor still holds equitable title, while the trustee holds legal title.

Defeasance

The process of releasing a borrower from its debt obligation (mortgage loan) and substituting the lien on the property with acceptable replacement collateral (typically treasury bonds). This replacement collateral is expected to generate a comparable substitute cash flow, which would otherwise be required on the existing debt were it not prepaid.

Delaware Statutory Trust

A distinct legal entity used by real estate investors seeking to defer their capital gains taxes through the use of a 1031 tax deferred exchange. The primary advantage of the DST is the trust's ability to obtain favorable financing terms compared to other ownership structures (such as "Tenants in Common") because the lender views the entity as only one borrower.

Design Architect

Design architect role is to create the design concepts of a building within the parameters created by the site, environment, budget and other factors. While they create the vision and refine the project down to specificity, the design architect does not prepare the construction documents or put their name on and certify the Construction Documents, nor do they provide construction administration.

Design Development

The period following schematic design whereby all design team consultants work together to further refine the project details. In this phase, the design team begins to select systems and materials and looks carefully at the coordination of all the components. The team will start to develop construction details and produce more refined graphical representations of the project. Typical items produced during this phase are detailed plans, sections, and elevations; schedules; and MEP specs. The architect may produce material boards showing various finishes, materials and colors that will be utilized in the development. The structural engineers, among other things, get specific with laying out and sizing structural components. The MEP engineers go into more details with equipment sizing and layouts. Many other design consultants are also contributing and working together with the architect and the owner in preparation of moving to into the Construction Documents phase.

Development Spread

The difference, denoted in basis points, between the market cap rate and the yield-on-cost. The Development Spread measures the "development pop," or value added by taking on the construction and lease-up risk. The greater the development spread, the more likely a development project will be deemed financially feasible.

Think of it in these terms. A real estate investor has the option to either a) acquire a fully built and stabilized asset at some market cap rate or b) construct and lease-up a brand-new property at some yield-on-cost. In order to make the latter worthwhile, a benefit commensurate with the risk must be gained, otherwise there is no incentive to take on the development risk. One way the developer and its capital partners measure the potential benefit is by looking at the difference in yield between the two options, or the Development Spread.

Development Yield

A metric used in real estate development, Development Yield is calculated as the project's net operating income (or sometimes cash flow from operations) at stabilization divided by the total project cost. Development Yield is also referred to as a project's Yield-on-Cost.

Direct Capitalization

A valuation method common to real estate where the value of an income-producing property is calculated by taking its stabilized net operating income and divided that by a market capitalization rate. Direct Capitalization (or "direct cap") analysis assumes that the income and expenses used in the calculation are perpetual.

Value of Income-Producing Real Estate = Stabilized Net Operating Income ÷ Market Capitalization Rate

Discount Rate

The rate at which future cash flows are discounted. We discount the value of money that is expected to be earned further out in the future because it is less certain that we will receive it. So, a dollar earned is worth less and less the further out in the future we expect to earn it. The decrease in value is determined by the discount rate we apply over the hold period. The discounted values in each period are then added together to create a present value of an asset in a discounted cash flow (DCF) model. In real estate valuation models, the discount rate can be interpreted as the Cap Rate plus expected NOI growth, representing the income and growth components of the total required rate of return, respectively.

Discounted Cash Flow

An investment analysis tool used regularly by real estate professionals to make buy, sell, hold, and development investment decisions. The discounted cash flow (DCF) is a process by which the real estate professional forecasts the future cash flows of an investment (rents, expenses, CapEx, debt service, sale price, etc.), and then discounts those cash flows to the present to arrive at time value of money return metrics such as internal rate of return and net present value.

The estimated cash flows from the DCF can also be used to calculate other risk and return metrics such as debt service coverage ratio, breakeven occupancy, debt yield, cash-on-cash return, equity multiple, etc., as well as to perform other analyses such as sensitivity analysis.

Draw

A periodic disbursement from the lender to the borrower from the construction loan proceeds to cover costs incurred during the development process. Common costs include materials, contractors or subcontractors, or any other vendor invoices in a given period during the development process. Typically, draws are monthly.

Draw Schedule

The construction draw schedule details how construction loan proceeds are anticipated to be used/disbursed over the loan period, specifically for what purpose and at what point in the development project. Construction loans are not immediately advanced when the loan closes. Instead, the lender will require a detailed property budget and agree to advance funds as certain milestones or completion percentages are achieved for the project, which becomes the draw schedule.

DSC

Debt Service Coverage. See Debt Service Coverage Ratio.

DSCR

See Debt Service Coverage Ratio.

DST

See Delaware Statutory Trust.

Duration

See Mortgage Loan Duration.

Earnest Money Deposit

An initial deposit paid by a property buyer as a show of good faith to the seller. The money is typically held in escrow by a title company, lawyer, or any escrow agent agreed upon between the buyer and seller, until the transaction closes and all suspensive conditions have been fulfilled, following which the earnest money is used to offset the initial purchase price paid by the buyer. However, if the seller defaults and the deal falls through then the deposit is returned to the buyer.

Earn-Out

A provision within a loan agreement that allows the borrower to receive additional funds from the lender upon completion of certain events (such as receiving a Certificate of Occupancy or surpassing pre-defined operating performance thresholds). Earn-outs are structured using holdback agreements.

Easement

An easement gives an individual or entity the legal right to use or access the property owned by some other individual or entity. Common instances for easements grant public access for roads or access to utility companies to install or maintain gas and power lines or other cables running through the property.

Economic Vacancy

The difference between the gross potential rent at a property and the actual rent collected. An example of this would be an apartment complex with a 2-week preparation period for new tenants and a 50% annual tenant turnover. Assuming the property was 100% occupied (or a physical vacancy of 0%), there would still be an economic vacancy of 1.92% (2/52 weeks x 50%) whereby the property owner would only receive 98.08% of his annual cash flow.

Effective Gross Revenue

Also referred to as Effective Gross Income, EGR, or EGI. Effective Gross Revenue is the sum of total Rental Revenue and total Other Income, less any adjustment for general vacancy and credit loss.

Effective Gross Revenue = Total Rental Revenue + Total Other Income - General Vacancy

EGR

See Effective Gross Revenue.

Elevation

An architectural drawing that depicts an object in two dimensions and from a front, side, or rear vantage point

EMx

Common abbreviation for Equity Multiple.

Entitlement Process

The process through which a real estate developer or landowner seeks the right to develop (or redevelop) property with government approvals for zoning, density, design, use, and occupancy permits. Upon securing all necessary entitlements from the applicable jurisdiction(s), the real estate developer is thus entitled to build what was proposed and approved.

Environmental Site Assessment

The Environmental Site Assessment (ESA), also known as a Phase I ESA, researches the current and historical uses of a property and identifies any subsequent environmental impacts of which an investor would want to be aware. The ESA will look at the site's and adjacent sites' current and historical uses, impacts on soil or groundwater, compliance with all regulatory databases, especially as it relates to hazardous material that may be stored on the site through under- or above-ground storage tanks (USTs and ASTs) or that may exist otherwise. The ESA will commonly also include testing for asbestos, lead-based paint, mold, lead in drinking water, and radon. Investors will assess the risk and may require further remedies to issues appearing on the ESA before closing and may require a Phase II ESA to provide further testing at the site. Particular concerns to investors on the ESA would be the past or current existence of dry cleaners, gas stations, auto repair shops and various manufacturing sites that may impact the property.

Equitable Title

Equitable title and legal title are like two parts to a complete title. Equitable title gives an entity beneficial interest in the property or the full use and enjoyment of the property. Legal title provides enforceable legal ownership in court. Legal title is commonly used as collateral when there is debt on a property.

When a loan is secured through a mortgage, either the borrower maintains legal title and the lender places a mortgage lien on the property (lien theory states) or the lender takes legal title, while the borrower has equitable title (title theory states). If the borrower is in default with a mortgage the lender has to go through the courts to foreclose. When the loan is secured through a deed of trust, legal title is given to a neutral third party, or trustee, and the lender can usually foreclose on the property without going to court.

Equity Multiple

A return metric which shows how much an investor earned on his or her invested capital. The equity multiple (EMx) is calculated by dividing the sum of all capital inflows (capital distributions) by the sum of all capital outflows (capital contributions). While the equity multiple does not account for the time value of money, it does describe the total cash returned to the investor and is thus often utilized alongside the internal rate of return in real estate investment analysis.

The Equity Multiple is typically used in conjunction with other return metrics such as Internal Rate of Return, Cash-on-Cash Return, Free and Clear Return, and Average Rate of Return, among others. The equity multiple can be calculated before and after taxes and on an unlevered (without debt) or on a levered (with debt) basis.

ESA
See Environmental Site Assessment.

Estoppel
See Tenant Estoppel Certificate.

European-style Waterfall
A common method for distributing investment cash flow between two or more partners. A European-style waterfall refers to a form of equity waterfall where no promote (i.e., carried interest) is paid to the sponsor (i.e., general partner) until the limited partner has received a full return of capital and earned a preferred return. Distributable cash flow during operations and distributable cash flow at a capital event are largely treated the same.

While referred to as European-style, this form of real estate partnership waterfall is common worldwide, including in the United States. It is often preferred by limited partners as it reduces the probability that promote distributions made to the GP must be clawed back at a later due date. It is most common to partnerships with institutional partners.

Expansion Rights
The legal right given by a landlord to a tenant to occupy additional leasable area in a building. These rights constrain the landlord's ability to lease the building and are thus typically only seen when tenants have a high degree of negotiation leverage.

Expense Stop

A mechanism in a lease whereby there is a fixed amount of operating expense that the landlord will pay for each year; above that, the tenant is responsible to pay. Thus, the landlord is responsible to pay for all operating expenses below the Expense Stop, while the tenant is responsible for any amount above the Expense Stop.

So, for example, if the Expense Stop is $10 per square foot and operating expenses in a given year equal $11 per square foot, the tenant would be responsible to reimburse the landlord $1 per square foot ($11 - $10).

Expense Stops can take the form of an agreed upon amount, typically expressed in an amount per square foot or per square meter or a base year stop. A base year stop sets the expense stop equal to the actual operating expenses in the first year of the lease. So, for instance, if the actual operating expenses in the first year amounted to $9.50 per square foot, the Expense Stop would be set at $9.50 per square foot and the tenant would be responsible to reimburse the landlord for any expenses above $9.50 per square foot in any subsequent year.

FAR

See Floor Area Ratio.

Factory Outlet

A factory outlet center is a retail subtype characterized for having outlet stores owned by manufacturers and retailers that sell brand-name discounted goods. Anchors for this subtype include those same manufacturers' and retailers' outlets (like major apparel or footwear companies). Factory outlets also serve a large trade area of 25 to 75 miles and average around 250,000 SF and larger in size.

Source: ICSC

FF&E
See Furniture, Fixtures, and Equipment.

FFO
See Funds from Operations.

Fee Simple
Fee simple is a form of ownership in real property. Specifically, it refers to an owner having full and irrevocable ownership of the land and any buildings on that land. Fee simple is the highest form of property ownership, and most real estate firms own real estate Fee Simple.

Festival Center
See Theme Retail Center.

Financing Memorandum
A request for mortgage financing given to lenders by commercial real estate borrowers (or their representatives) for the lenders' investment consideration. The memorandum will typically highlight various terms and

property specifics such as the borrower's requested loan terms, a detailed description of the property, the location and relevant demographic trends, a financial summary, pictures, comparable sales and/or rentals, and any other information pertinent to the investment. The Financing Memorandum is similar to the Offering Memorandum in format and content, but the offering is for a real estate debt rather than equity investment.

Fixed Costs

Costs that do not change based on of the property's level of occupancy or operation. For example, the landlord's monthly insurance premiums will generally remain fixed regardless of whether the property is 50% or 80% occupied. In some real estate financial models, the user is given the option to choose what percentage of a given expense is fixed with items such as insurance and taxes deserving 100% fixed treatment. This is in contrast to Variable Costs, which vary with the property's level of operation.

Fixed Price Contract

As it relates to commercial real estate, a fixed price contract is an agreement where a contractor presents a quote to the property owner or general contractor, with a predetermined value that does not change to perform the work of a contract. In these types of contracts, once the terms are agreed, the price to fulfill the contract does not change, regardless of whether the labor or material costs change throughout the term of the contract.

Fixed Rate Debt

Fixed Rate Debt refers to a form of financing where the interest rate used to calculate the interest due in each period is constant (i.e., does not change). This is in contrast to Floating Rate debt, where the interest rate does change periodically.

The interest rate on a fixed rate loan is set (i.e., locked) upon origination of the loan. The interest rate is generally determined by taking some benchmark rate (e.g., government bonds) and adding a premium to that rate to arrive at the fixed annual interest rate.

So for instance, imagine a lender is pricing a 10-yr fixed rate loan using the 10-yr UST as the benchmark. Furthermore, imagine the lender quotes the rate at 150 bps over the 10-yr UST. At the time of the rate lock, the lender will take the yield on the 10-yr UST at that moment (e.g., 1.60%) and will add the agreed upon premium (150 bps or 1.50%) to arrive at the fixed interest rate (1.60% + 1.50% = 3.10%).

Floating Rate Debt

Floating Rate or Variable Rate debt, refers to a form of financing where the interest rate used to calculate the interest due in each period changes (i.e., varies or floats) periodically. The interest rate for a floating rate loan is generally calculated by taking a regularly changing benchmark rate (e.g., LIBOR, SOFR, government bonds, etc.) and adding some premium to that rate to arrive at a periodic interest rate. Floating Rate debt is in contrast to Fixed Rate debt, where the interest rate does not change.

So for instance, imagine that the annual interest rate on a floating rate loan is calculated each month by taking the one-month LIBOR and adding 200 bps (i.e., 2.00%) to arrive at the periodic interest rate. If in month one the one-month LIBOR was 0.50%, then the annual interest rate for purposes of calculating the interest due in month one would be equal to 0.50% + 2.00% = 2.50%.

Further imagine that from month one to month two, the LIBOR rate increased from 0.50% to 0.60%. For purposes of calculating interest in month two, the annual interest rate would increase from 2.50% to 2.60% (0.60% + 2.00%).

Floor Area Ratio

A ratio expressing the relationship between a building's floor area (currently built or permitted) and the land on which the property is located. A higher FAR ratio indicates a higher density (i.e., the more square feet legally permissible to be built on the land). For example, if a plot of land is 10,000 SF and there is a FAR of 6, then the allowable buildable square footage is 60,000 (10,000 x 6).

Floor Plan

An architectural drawing that depicts a floor layout of a specific floor or room of a building in two dimensions and from a top looking down vantage point.

Floor Plate

A term commonly used in commercial real estate to refer to an entire floor of a building. The term is commonly used when discussing square footage and/or variations in size and shape of floors within a building.

Example: There are two different floor plates in this building that should accommodate various users. The bottom third of the tower has 30,000 GSF floor plates that are rectangular, while the upper two thirds of the building consist of 20,000 GSF floor plates that are square.

Floor to Ceiling Height

The height between each floor plate in a building measured from the top of a floor to the surface of the ceiling.

Floor to Floor Height

The height between each floor plate in a building measured from the top of a floor to the top of the above floor.

Forward Sale

A binding contract between two parties to enter into a purchase and sale agreement at a fixed future date, the terms and conditions of which are agreed upon today.

Free and Clear Return

The total unlevered (before debt) pre-tax cash flow of a real estate project divided by the total capital invested, generally expressed as a percentage on an annual basis.

To clarify, the numerator is typically total unlevered pre-tax cash flow in a given year, while the denominator contains the total amount of capital invested assuming there is no debt. While the Free and Clear Return does not account for taxes and does not take into account the time value of money, it is a useful screening tool used by investors when evaluating potential investments. The Free and Clear Return is the unlevered equivalent of the Cash-on-Cash Return, and thus sometimes referred to as the Unlevered Cash-on-Cash Return.

The Free and Clear Return of an investment is especially important to core investment strategy investors more interested in stable cash flow than in asset appreciation. The Free and Clear Return is typically used alongside other return metrics such as the Equity Multiple and Internal Rate of Return to appropriately assess an investment.

Front-load

Front-load warehouses have the loading docks on the front of the building, in relation to the street from which trucks enter.

Full-Service Gross Lease

A commercial lease where the tenant pays a base rent and the landlord pays for all operating expenses related to the tenant's occupancy of the space, such as common area maintenance, utilities, property insurance, and property taxes. FSG leases contrast with net leases, wherein the tenant pays for some or all operating expenses.

Full-Service Hotel

A hotel that has a dedicated food and beverage (F&B) component and offers a full range of amenities and services, such as concierge service, bars and restaurants, pool and spa, etc. Full-service hotels have high fixed costs and appeal to the more affluent casual and business travelers who are able to afford the higher-than-average room rate.

Funds from Operations

A widely accepted metric used to analyze the performance of a REIT. Funds from Operations, or FFO, accounts for the fact that net income on a REIT's income statement may be an inaccurate representation of the REIT's true performance. As such, net income is adjusted as follows to arrive at FFO:

FFO = Net Income + Depreciation + Amortization − Gain/Loss on Sale of Properties

Funds from Operations is comparable to the Cash Flow from Operations metric, which is used in analyzing individual properties.

Furniture, Fixtures, and Equipment

Furniture, Fixtures, and Equipment (FF&E). In real estate financial analysis, FF&E is most often found as a line item in development budgets and operating statements. It can generally be defined as any easily moveable object not permanently affixed to the building. Examples of FF&E include the following: chairs, beds, couches, curtains, desks, sconces, tables.

Future Value Factor

Also called the Future Amount of One or FV Factor, the Future Value Factor is a formula used to calculate the Future Value of 1 unit today, n number of periods into the future. The FV Factor is equal to $(1 + i)^n$ where i is the rate (e.g., interest rate or discount rate) and n is the number of periods. So, for example at a 12% interest rate, $1 USD invested today would be worth $(1 + 12\%)^5$ or $1.7623 USD five years from now.

One use for the FV Factor in real estate is to estimate future rent based on today's rent, grown at some growth rate. So if an apartment unit rents for $1,000 per month today and rent is expected to grow 3% per year for the next five years, five years from now that same apartment unit will be expected to rent for $(1+3\%)^5$ * $1,000 or $1,159.27 per month.

The FV Factor is the inverse of the related PV Factor or Present Value Factor.

Garden Apartment

Low-rise apartments set on a sizable, landscaped plot and typically operate under a single management. They are characterized by being surrounded with lawns, trees, and gardens. These apartment subtypes will most likely offer access to a backyard patio and are pet friendly.

Source: NCREIF

General Contractor

An entity that oversees the execution of a construction project on behalf of the ownership of a property. The General Contractor manages the day-to-day operations on site and oversees all the subcontractors.

General Vacancy and Credit Loss

In real estate underwriting, General Vacancy and Credit Loss is an adjustment to Gross Potential Income (Rental Revenue + Other Income) on the pro forma income statement. It is used to factor in likely vacancy loss due to market conditions and expected credit loss due to tenants' failure to pay.

General Warranty Deed

Common in residential real estate and not generally used in commercial real estate, a general warranty deed guarantees that the seller has the right to sell the property and that it is free of any encumbrances such as debt, liens, or any adverse claims. A general warranty allows the grantee, or new owner of the property, the ability to sue the grantor for damages if any such legitimate challenges to title or unknown encumbrances emerge.

GMP
See Guaranteed Maximum Price.

Good News Money
Additional funds paid out to the borrower by a mortgage lender upon the occurrence of certain "good news" events, such as the owner concluding a lease agreement with a major tenant in the building or reaching some pre-determined net operating income. Such additional funds, commonly referred to as an "earn-out," are added to the outstanding loan balance and are generally subject to the same terms as the underlying loan.

Grantee
In a real estate sale transaction, a grantee is the buyer of the property. In a sale transaction, the grantor conveys, or transfers, title through a deed to the grantee.

Grantor
In a real estate sale transaction, a grantor is the seller of the property. In a sale transaction, the grantor conveys, or transfers, title through a deed to the grantee.

Gross Absorption
Gross absorption is measured as the total amount of space (or number of units for residential) leased in a given period divided by the total amount of space (or number of units) in a defined market. Gross absorption can be a misleading metric because it doesn't take into account vacancies. To

get a more complete picture of the strength or weakness of market leasing, one should look to the net absorption metric. To elaborate, imagine if a market with a total of 100 units had leased 10 units. The gross absorption rate would be 10%. However, what if in that same period, one of two scenarios happened. In scenario 1, 10 units vacated, but in scenario 2, 0 units vacated. If there were zero units that were vacated, this would indicate a strong market absorption, but if there were 10 units that vacated, this may indicate that the market is stagnant. We capture this issue of vacated units in the net absorption metric thus it is a more comprehensive metric for understanding a market's current condition.

Gross Asset Value

A measure used to describe the market value of a property. The value includes debt and equity positions but excludes any acquisition/closing costs.

Ground Lease

A lease structure where a real estate investor rents the land (i.e., ground) only. In the case of a ground lease, generally one party owns the land (a fee simple interest) while a separate party owns the improvements (a leasehold interest). In most cases, the owner of the land leases the land to the owner of the improvements for an extended period of time (20 - 100 years).

When the ground lease predates a mortgage on the leasehold interest, the ground lease generally has priority over that mortgage unless the ground lease is expressly subordinated to the mortgage. Thus, a ground lease is often thought of and valued as a form of financing.

The ground lease is a common vehicle used by generational families to generate cash flow from well-located parcels of land without having to operate the property nor give up ownership in the property. For instance, the Martinez family owns a 10-acre parcel at the corner of main and main. They lease the parcel for $100,000 per year to Jennifer's Bakery for 50 years, who in turn builds a bakery on the property. Jennifer's Bakery operates a bakery on the property for the next 50 years and, at the end of the ground lease term, returns the land together with any improvements on the land to the Martinez Family.

Guarantee of Non-Recourse Carveouts

Also referred to as a "Bad-Boy Guarantee," a Guarantee of Non-Recourse Carveouts is a guarantee provided by an individual or entity which covers the extent of the recourse liability arising from any non-recourse carveout. These are commonly required when an individual entity is not guaranteeing the loan.

Guaranteed Maximum Price

A type of cost plus contract whereby the contractor is reimbursed for all construction related costs, plus a fixed fee. The agreed upon costs and fee are capped, transferring the risk of cost overruns to the contractor, whilst any savings resulting from cost underruns may either be a point of negotiation between the general contractor and the owner or completely realized by the project owner.

Hangout and Hangout Risk

The hangout is the expected outstanding loan balance owed the lender by the borrower at the end of the lease term of a key tenant, while the hangout risk is the risk to the lender associated with the borrower's ability or inability to repay said loan. An especially important consideration in investments with a single tenant, the hangout risk is determined by comparing the hangout to the dark value (value of the vacant real estate) to determine whether the borrower will be able to repay the loan. This risk can be quantified by dividing the hangout by the dark value.

For example, a borrower secures a $100,000, 20-year loan against a property leased to WalBlues for 15 years. At the end of year 15, the outstanding loan balance is expected to be $50,000. The lender projects the value of the vacant property in year 15 to be $50,000. Therefore, the hangout risk is high, as represented by the expected LTV at the end of the lease term ($50,000 ÷ $50,000 = 100%), since the borrower will need to re-lease the property before year 20 to be able to refinance the property to repay the lender.

Hard Costs

Any development costs associated with the physical construction of a building. These costs are easy to quantify and typically include items such as raw materials, labor, and interior finish, etc. Hard costs are also referred to as Direct Costs.

Hectare

A unit of land that equals 10,000 square meters or 107,639 square feet.

Hold/Sell Analysis

The process of analyzing whether to continue holding (i.e., owning) income-producing real estate, or whether to sell the real estate and reinvest the proceeds in an alternative opportunity. Many professional real estate asset and portfolio managers perform this analysis on a regular basis, so as to optimize the overall returns of their respective portfolios and beat their target benchmarks.

Real estate professionals use analysis tools such as real estate discounted cash flow models to calculate the return on the *hold scenario* and then compare that to the projected returns on the *sell and reinvest scenario* to make a more informed investment decision.

Holdback

A holdback is a portion of commercial loan proceeds that are retained by the lender until certain objectives have been met. These objectives may include conditions like a certain percentage of development has been completed or a certain NOI is achieved at the property. Holdback proceeds are generally held in an escrow account.

Hotel "Flag"

An informal term used to denote an operating brand within the hotel industry. Marriott, Hilton, and Best Western are examples of "Flags" used by owners of hotel properties.

HUD Home

A residential property owned by the Department of Housing and Development (HUD). If a foreclosed home was acquired using proceeds from an FHA-insured loan, the FHA will pay out the lender for the balance due and ownership of the property will transfer to HUD.

In arrears

To pay for services after the work has been done.

Income Approach

One of three appraisal methods used in commercial real estate to estimate the value of income-producing property. The Income Approach includes two methods. The first method, the Income Capitalization Method, is a process whereby one year's Net Operating Income is divided by a market Capitalization Rate to arrive at an estimated value. The second method uses the Discounted Cash Flow to calculate the present value of a real estate investment's forecasted future income and reversion value. The Income Approach is the most common appraisal method used to evaluate income-producing real estate.

Inducement

See Concessions.

Industrial Flex

An industrial building that can typically be adapted for a wide variety of uses. This may include office space, as well as retail, distribution, or a variety of industrial uses.

In-place Rent

See also Contract Rent. In-place Rent is the rent being charged/collected on existing leases at a property. In contrast to Market Rent, in-place rent is not based on market conditions but rather is based on the lease contract signed between the landlord and tenant.

Institutional Investor

An institutional real estate investor is a large company or organization with substantial capital and an allocation to real estate investments. Pension funds, life insurance companies, investment banks, sovereign wealth funds, and endowments are examples of institutional investors. Most often, the institutional investor act as the limited partner in a real estate partnership, providing equity capital while relying on the general partner (sponsor) for geographic and property-type expertise. Given their size and ready access to the capital markets, institutional investors tend to have a lower cost of capital than their non-institutional counterparts, allowing them to pay more for real estate assets.

Interest Reserve

A reserve account held by the lender of a construction loan and used by the borrower to cover loan interest shortfalls during construction and lease-up. The interest reserve is funded via the initial proceeds from the construction loan and is calculated based either on expected future draws or by means of a simple average estimate of the outstanding loan balance throughout the loan period.

Internal Rate of Return

The discount rate at which the net present value of an investment is equal to zero. The internal rate of return is a time value of money metric, representing the true annual rate of earnings on an investment. In real estate practice, IRR is used together with other return metrics such as equity multiple, cash-on-cash return, and average rate of return to compare real estate investments and make investment decisions.

Unlevered IRR or unleveraged IRR is the internal rate of return of a string of cash flows without financing.

Levered IRR or leveraged IRR is the internal rate of return of a string of cash flows with financing included.

The Internal Rate of Return is arrived at by using the same formula used to calculate net present value *(NPV)*, but by setting net present value to zero and solving for discount rate *r*. In Excel, IRR can be calculated by using the IRR(), XIRR(), or MIRR() functions.

IRR

See Internal Rate of Return.

Jingle Mail

A colloquialism in real estate, Jingle Mail is the letter a lender would receive containing a borrower's keys (making a "jingle" sound as the keys bounced around). This situation typically occurs when there is a sharp decrease in the market value of a property, such as occurred during the 2008 subprime mortgage crisis. Jingle Mail generally refers to a Deed in Lieu of Foreclosure and in many parts of the world is also called "giving back the keys."

Joint Tenancy

An ownership of real property by two or more people whereby if one person dies, the ownership held by the deceased passes on to the surviving owners.

Key Money

Money provided by a hotel operator or hotel "flag" to a hotel owner in order to secure a hotel management or franchise agreement at a hotel property. In highly competitive hotel markets, where operators are looking to get a foothold or expand their brand, operators may use key money as one negotiating tool and will compensate the hotel owner as part of the agreement.

Key money is especially relevant in hotel development projects where risks are particularly high and lenders may be much more conservative for this risky asset class.

Key Performance Indicator

A metric used to measure the performance of a property. Real estate specific KPI's include metrics such as Cap Rate, LTV, Debt Yield, Cash on Cash Return, Internal Rate of Return, and Equity Multiple, among others.

Land Assemblage

A tactic employed in land acquisition, where a real estate professional acquires two or more adjacent parcels, combining them into one. Land assemblage can be a time-consuming, complicated process, with the complexity increasing exponentially depending on the number of parcels and landowners. However, the complex process is worth it when the value of the whole (the combined parcels) is greater than the sum of the value of the parts (the individual parcels).

For example, a residential real estate developer acquires four 50-acre parcels, from four different owners, each worth $100,000, for a total cost of $400,000 (4 x $100,000

= $400,000). After assembling the 200 acres (50 acres x 4), the new single parcel is worth $500,000.

Land Use Restriction Agreements

An agreement between a property owner and the government whereby the property owner agrees to limit the use of its property in exchange for some pre-determined tax credits or bond financings. A Land Use Restriction Agreement (LURA) is most common to low income housing tax credits (LIHTC) where the property owner agrees to limit the rent it may charge at the property and in so doing becomes eligible for certain tax credits.

The LURA stays with the land, meaning any restrictions defined in the agreement continue on even after a sale. These restrictions generally last for a pre-defined period of time, usually 15 to 30 years depending on the agreement and jurisdiction.

Lease Depth

The distance measured between the building window line and the building core wall's exterior side.

Leasehold Interest

In real estate, a leasehold interest refers to a structure where an individual or entity (lessee) leases the land (i.e., ground lease) from the fee simple owner (lessor) of the land for an extended period of time. The lessee of a leasehold estate will generally own the improvements on the land and use the land and improvements as if the lessee were the owner of the land. During the term of the ground lease, the lessee will pay rent to the lessor for use of the land. At the end of the ground lease term, the lessee must return use of the land, and any improvements thereon, to the landowner.

Real estate investors are willing to lease the land when the cash flow from the improvements alone, after paying the ground lease payment, make the investment feasible. This is common with high-quality locations where the leasehold owner wants the location but the land owner is only willing to lease the land rather than sell it.

Many office buildings in gateway cities (e.g. New York) are leasehold estates where the owner of the building leases the land underneath the building from a separate individual or entity for an extended period of time. One such example is the World Trade Center in New York City. The land is owned by the Port Authority of New York and New Jersey but controlled by a separate group under a 99-year ground lease originally executed in July 2001.

Leasing Commissions

A commission, generally paid by the landlord to a leasing broker, for procuring a tenant for a rentable piece of real estate. Leasing Commissions are typically paid at the start of the lease and are commonly paid both when a new tenant occupies a space and when an existing tenant renews its lease. While Leasing Commission rates vary by market, they're generally quoted as a percentage of the total rent over the term of the lease (e.g., 6%).

Legal Title

Equitable title and legal title are like two parts to a complete title. Equitable title gives an entity beneficial interest in the property for the full use and enjoyment of the property. Legal title provides enforceable legal ownership in court. Legal title is commonly used as collateral when there is debt on a property.

When a loan is secured through a mortgage, either the borrower maintains legal title and the lender places a mortgage lien on the property (lien theory states) or the lender takes legal title, while the borrower has equitable title (title theory states). If the borrower is in default, with a mortgage the lender has to go through the courts to foreclose. When the loan is secured through a deed of trust, legal title is given to a neutral third party, or trustee, and the borrower can usually foreclose on the property without going to court.

Lessee

Someone who leases or rents space.

Someone who pays rent to the owner or lessor in order to occupy a space.

Lessor

An entity that owns and leases a property to a tenant or lessee.

Letter of Intent

A non-binding legal document used to communicate the high-level business terms in a real estate transaction. The letter of intent, or LOI, is most often used by the buyer at the early stages of a real estate purchase. The buyer sends a "letter" to the seller conveying the terms under which the buyer would proceed with the acquisition of a seller's property.

Terms outlined in a letter of intent generally include purchase price, amount and treatment of earnest money, timing of closing, the condition of the property upon closing, and other high-level business terms the seller and buyer must agree to before drafting the lengthier, and binding, purchase and sale agreement (PSA).

Levered Cash Flow

The net cash inflows and outflows of a real estate investment taking into account cash flows related to financing. Levered cash flows generally consist of total investment costs, loan fundings and payoffs, net operating cash flows after financing, and asset reversion cash flows (i.e., net proceeds from sale). In real estate financial analysis, the levered cash flow line is used to calculate the levered internal rate of return and levered equity multiple of a prospective real estate investment.

Lien Theory States

Lien theory states are those states in which the title remains with the borrower in a lending scenario. The lender instead holds a lien on the property via the mortgage, which gives it a right of possession until the borrower pays off the loan balance.

Life Plan Community

See Continuing Care Retirement Communities (CCRCs).

Lifestyle Retail Center

Lifestyle retail centers provide dining and entertainment in outdoor settings with upscale national-chain specialty stores. They tend to be over 300,000 SF in size, with a trade area of 8 to 12 miles. Large format upscale specialty is the most common type of anchor tenant for this retail subtype.

Source: ICSC

Limited Partner

A limited partner is a passive (in terms of management responsibility) partner in a real estate investment. In a typical real estate partnership, the general partner (sponsor or GP) manages the day-to-day aspects of the investment strategy and brings local and property type expertise. The limited partner (or partners) typically brings the majority of the equity capital and only weighs in on critical decisions.

Limited-Service Hotel

A hotel that provides only the basic amenities and services such as a swimming pool and/or business center. Limited-service hotels (such as Fairfield Inn or Homewood Suites) operate on smaller budgets, enabling them to pass on the cost savings to travelers via lower room rates.

Limited Warranty Deed

See Special Warranty Deed.

Linear Mortgage

A mortgage loan where the amount of principal due in each period is static. As a result, the loan payment due in each period decreases over time as the amount of interest due decreases and the principal due stays the same. The loan balance likewise decreases in a straight-line (i.e., linear) fashion over the loan term.

Loan Amortization

The repayment of the principal balance of a loan through periodic payments over time. In an amortizing loan, a portion of the loan payment each period is used to pay the interest owed for that period with the balance used to pay down principal on the loan. Although the periodic loan payments remain constant throughout the loan term, the portion allocated to principal reduction increases over time as the principal balance is reduced. Thus, less interest is owed in each period.

Loan to Cost

In real estate, Loan to Cost (LTC) is the ratio of the outstanding loan balance to total project cost. The higher the LTC, the less cash equity the borrower has invested in the property (i.e., less "skin in the game") and therefore the higher the risk that the borrower will default on the loan. Real estate lenders most often use this metric in assessing the risk of lending on a real estate development project, but LTC is also considered on acquisition loans to compare the proposed loan amount to the acquisition price.

Loan to Cost (LTC) = Loan Amount / Total Project Cost

Loan to Value

In real estate, Loan to Value (LTV) is the ratio of the outstanding loan balance to the value of the property expressed as a percentage. The higher the LTV, the higher the risk is that the borrower will be able to repay the loan at maturity. Higher LTV's usually correlate with higher interest rates as well to account for the additional risk. Real estate lenders use this important metric, together with debt yield and debt service coverage ratio, among others, to assess the risk of a loan and arrive at an appropriate loan amount.

Loan to Value (LTV) = Loan Amount / Property Value

Load Factor

Rentable area / usable area = load factor

Example: If a building has 50,000 sf of rentable area and 40,000 sf of usable area, the building has a load factor of 1.25 (50,000/40,000).

Loan Workout

A resolution agreed upon between the lender and the borrower to restructure the terms of the loan before foreclosure of the property. Workouts typically involve negotiations regarding the minimum monthly payment and/or the amortization period. In some cases, a loan workout results in the borrower "giving back the keys" rather than the lender formally foreclosing on the property.

Lock Out

A common clause in a CRE loan agreement. This is the period of time after disbursement that a borrower is not allowed to prepay the loan. Lenders will many times enforce a lock out period, along with prepayment penalties after the lock out period, as a way to ensure they are receiving earnings off the money they are responsible for disbursing.

Lock Out Period

See Lock Out.

Loss-to-Lease

The difference between in-place rent (or contract rent) and market rent. The loss-to-lease concept is most often used in multifamily underwriting. Because contractual lease rates lag the actual market, the loss-to-lease metric acts to help the real estate professional forecast coming changes to actual income going forward.

LTC

See Loan to Cost.

LTV

See Loan to Value.

Lump Sum Contract

A contract whereby the total price of an entire construction project is negotiated and agreed to between the General Contractor (GC) and the Owner, regardless of what the actual price ends up being at the end of the project. This type of contract shifts all risks (future price increases) and rewards (potential future cost savings) onto the contractor. To further clarify, if the actual costs of construction are above the lump sum, the contractor bears the cost; if the actual costs end up being below the lump sum, the GC will still get paid the lump sum and earn the difference. This type of contract is common when there is a clearly defined scope of work and costs can be reasonably estimated or if the GC has a reason to believe they can keep costs under control and under budget.

LURA

See Land Use Restriction Agreements.

Make Ready Costs

Most often seen on multifamily operating statements, 'Make Ready' costs refer to minor repairs and maintenance work to an apartment unit in order to ensure that the unit is in a suitable condition before being placed on the market and leased to a subsequent tenant. Activities included in this process range from cleaning services and painting to countertop resurfacing and trash removal.

Market Rent

The rent a typical tenant would pay for a comparable unit or suite in the same or comparable market. A real estate owner will often compare the average contract rental rate at their property to the market rent in the area to determine whether there is potential to increase rents at the real estate owner's property.

Master Tenant

A tenant who leases directly from the property owner and subsequently subleases all (or a portion of) the property to other tenants.

MEP

MEP is a common acronym for mechanical, electrical, plumbing and simply refers to these respective systems of a building collectively.

MEP Engineer

The mechanical, electrical, and plumbing systems expert. These engineers lead the design and implementation of these systems throughout the construction process, serving as the central resource during the building's development. Systems also under an MEP engineer's purview may also include fire suppression systems, sustainable building designs, and automation systems.

Metropolitan Statistical Area

A Metropolitan Statistical Area, or MSA, is an area that usually includes a major city at its core and the surrounding towns and suburbs. It is not a legal area that is governed by any one entity, but an area to which numerous towns and a city, or cities, have a lot of inter-connectivity.

Mezzanine Debt

In real estate, mezzanine debt, or *mezz*, is a subordinate loan on real property secured by an interest in the entity that owns the real property rather than on the real property itself. In the event of default, because the entity rather than the real estate acts as collateral, the mezzanine lender is able to foreclose on the entity via a UCC foreclosure - a faster and less expensive process than a foreclosure on the real estate would be. In the capital stack, mezzanine debt falls between mortgage debt and equity. It carries a higher interest rate than more senior debt due to its riskier place in the capital stack.

Mill

A "mill" is 1/1,000 of a dollar, or $1 for each $1,000 of assessed value. A mill is used to calculate a property's millage rate.

Millage Rate

The millage rate is used to calculate the property tax on real property. This is calculated in increments of $1,000, with each mill representing 0.1% of the property's taxed assessed value, which is often lower than market value. For example, if a property's tax assessed value is $20,000,000 and has a millage rate of 20, then its property tax would equate to $400,000 ($20 for every $1,000 of value). In many jurisdictions, the millage rate is converted to a percentage (mill rate ÷ 1000) and quoted as a *property tax rate* for ease of calculation.

MHC

See Manufactured Housing Community.

MOIC

Abbreviation for Multiple on Invested Capital. *See Equity Multiple for the definition.*

Monte Carlo Method

A technique used in Stochastic (i.e. Probabilistic) Analysis whereby the professional performs simulations that result in a range of outcomes due to the uncertain nature of the inputs.

This method involves repeatedly running simulations hundreds or thousands of times, recording the outcomes of each simulation, and then aggregating those outcomes to understand the mean (i.e. the average outcome), standard deviation (i.e. the dispersion of outcomes), minimum value, and maximum value of all of the outcomes.

Mortgage Loan Duration

The number of periods (most commonly denoted in years) that must pass for half of the time-weighted present value of the debt service payments to be paid. Duration is an important measure of interest rate risk.

The longer the Duration, the greater exposure the loan has to interest rate risk. To hedge against that risk, lenders will often pair the mortgage loan asset with a liability of similar Duration and size.

Mortgage Constant

A rate calculated by dividing the periodic loan payment by the initial loan amount. The Mortgage (or Loan) Constant is often used as a tool to efficiently calculate loan payments and is represented as a percentage. For instance, a mortgage loan with an annual payment of $16,000 and an initial loan balance of $250,000 has a Mortgage Constant of 6.40%. In an interest only loan, this metric would be the same as the interest rate where with an amortizing loan this would be different because there are principal payments included as well.

Lenders can use this to compare different loans and how quickly they get back their loan amount through regular payments.

Mortgagee

The lender or entity that lends money to a borrower (mortgagor) to buy real estate.

Mortgagor

The borrower or entity receiving the loan to buy real estate.

MSA

See Metropolitan Statistical Area.

Multiple on Invested Capital

Another term used for Equity Multiple. *See Equity Multiple for the definition.*

Muni Bond

See Municipal Bond

Municipal Bond

A municipal bond, colloquially referred to as a muni bond, is a debt instrument originated by a state or local government for financing public projects. These bonds are generally exempt from federal as well as state and local taxes. As a result, investors demand a lower yield relative to bonds that are not tax-exempt.

Municipal bond yields are often used in real estate analysis to determine the appropriate discount rate for valuing a property tax abatement.

Negative Covenant

A type of restrictive property covenant that prohibits the landowner from certain acts. This type of covenant also runs with the land, remaining with any subsequent landowners. An example of a negative covenant may prohibit the landowner from expanding the physical building and increasing its square footage beyond a certain limit.

Neighborhood Center

Neighborhood retail centers are also convenience-related and typically have just one anchor, usually grocery or drug stores. A neighborhood center is around 75,000 SF with a trade area of 3 miles.

Source: ICSC

NER

See Net Effective Rent

Net Absorption

In the case of for lease property, net absorption is the rate at which rentable area is leased up over a period of time in a given market. The net absorption figure considers construction of new space, demolition of existing space and any additional vacancies during that period. It is often used to forecast demand and supply trends and is thus a key indicator for both property owners and developers, significantly influencing their pricing and timing decisions.

Net Effective Rent

The gross amount of rent payable by a tenant less any costs incurred by the landlord in order to lease the space to the tenant. Such costs typically include leasing commissions, tenant improvements and/or rent-free periods. So, for instance, imagine a tenant agrees to pay $720,000 in total rent over a three-year term and is offered $50,000 in concessions (e.g., tenant improvement allowance and free rent) and a $20,000 commission due to a leasing broker. The net effective rent is $720,000 - ($50,000 + $20,000) = $650,000 with a net effective monthly rent of $650,000 ÷ 36 = $18,055.55/month (vs. $20,000/month gross).

Net Lease

A commercial lease where the tenant pays base rent plus pays for its pro rata share of some or all operating expenses related to the tenant's occupancy of the space. Types of net leases include single net, double net, triple net, and absolute triple net. Expenses may be billed directly to the tenant, or the expenses may be paid by the landlord and reimbursed by the tenant. Net leases contrast with Gross Leases, wherein the landlord pays for all operating expenses.

Single Net (N): a net lease where the tenant pays base rent plus pays for one of the operating expense items such as common area maintenance (CAM), insurance, or property taxes

Double Net (NN): a net lease where the tenant pays base rent plus pays for property insurance and property taxes

Triple Net (NNN): a net lease where the tenant pays base rent plus pays for all operating expenses

Absolute Triple Net: a type of triple net lease where the tenant pays base rent, all operating expenses, plus pays a portion or all of the capital expenditures to maintain the condition property

Net Operating Income

The net income from a property, in a given period, after deducting operating expenses but before deducting capital expenditures, debt service, and taxes. To calculate Net Operating Income, the real estate professional subtracts operating expenses from effective gross income (Effective Gross Income - Operating Expenses = Net Operating Income). Net Operating Income (NOI) is arguably the most important income metric, as it is widely used to estimate the value of the property using the Income Capitalization Method.

NOI

See Net Operating Income.

Non-disclosure State

A state in the United States where the sales price of a sold property is not publicly available. In such situations, the sales value is estimated (for tax assessment and other purposes) using other metrics which are publicly available, such as the loan amount granted by the bank, or the mortgage transfer taxes paid.

Non-recourse Carveouts

Referred to colloquially as "Bad Boy Carveouts", a list of actions or guarantees that may result in the borrower or guarantor taking on partial or full recourse liability for the loan. These actions initially were limited in scope to "bad acts" such as theft or voluntary bankruptcy by the borrower. However, over time the list of non-recourse carveouts has grown to include acts which one may not consider wrongful (failing to permit property inspections or not paying real estate taxes).

Occupancy Cost

The total cost incurred by a tenant in order to occupy space in a building. These costs are all stipulated in the lease agreement and include items such as base rent, tenant reimbursement expenses, percentage rent, parking charges, etc.

Occupancy Cost Percentage

Also referred to as the tenant's Health Ratio, Occupancy Cost Percentage represents a tenant's total annual occupancy cost as a percentage of total annual tenant sales at the property. This metric is used by investors in retail real estate to better assess the financial health of the tenant at a given location. The lower the occupancy cost, the higher the probability the tenant will remain at the property long-term. The higher the occupancy cost, the more likely a tenant will vacate.

A healthy occupancy cost depends on the tenant type. While a healthy Occupancy Cost Percentage for a grocery tenant might be 2.5%, a similarly healthy Occupancy Cost Percentage for an apparel tenant might be 12%+. The variance in what is considered healthy largely depends on the profit margin of the products sold by the tenant. The higher the margin, the higher the occupancy cost a tenant can support.

OCIP

See Owner Controlled Insurance Program.

Offering Memorandum

A presentation and marketing document given to investors for their investment consideration summarizing a potential deal. The memorandum will typically highlight various aspects of the investment, such as a detailed description of the property, the location and relevant demographic trends, a financial summary, pictures, comparable sales and/or rentals, and any other information pertinent to the transaction. The Offering

Memorandum is similar to the Financing Memorandum in format and content, but the offering is for a real estate equity rather than debt investment.

OM

See Offering Memorandum.

Operating Expense Ratio

The ratio of Operating Expenses to Effective Gross Revenue. The Operating Expense ratio is a metric used in real estate underwriting to understand what proportion of gross revenue is used to cover the expenses necessary to operate the property. The amount leftover, after paying the operating expenses, is the Net Operating Income.

Operating Expense Ratio = Operating Expenses / Effective Gross Revenue

Operating Supplies and Equipment

OS&E is a common initialism used in the hotel industry for Operating Supplies and Equipment. OS&E refers to an enormous range of items that a hotel will need to operate. OS&E does not include items like stoves or washing machines or any major items that require installation. Examples of OS&E include the following: dishware, cutlery, trashcans, trays, cleaning supplies, staff uniforms, office supplies, irons and ironing boards, luggage carts, and vacuums.

Opportunistic

A real estate investment strategy categorized by high risk and high returns. Opportunistic real estate strategies typically involve a high degree of uncertainty and more volatility in cash flow and therefore require greater subject matter expertise. These strategies will often employ more leverage and subject the investors to a greater probability of losing their capital. Opportunistic real estate investments are most often either ground-up developments or the redevelopment of properties to a higher and better use.

Opportunity Zones

Opportunity Zones are special economic development zones created as part of the Tax Cuts and Jobs Act of 2017. Individuals and companies that invest in qualified opportunity zones enjoy special tax treatment to encourage investment in these distressed areas within the United States. The purpose of the creation of these zones, and the corresponding tax benefits of doing so, is meant to spur job growth and economic activity in these areas.

Individuals and companies that invest in opportunity zones can choose to temporarily defer tax on capital gains if those gains are invested in a qualified opportunity zone. For more information on the benefits and qualification for this program, view the IRS' Opportunity Zones Facts Sheet.

Option

See Option Agreement.

Option Agreement

An Option Agreement, or Option, is a formal agreement between a property owner and a potential buyer or lessee, in which the potential buyer or lessee usually pays the owner for the exclusive right to a negotiation in good faith or to allow the potential buyer or lessee to confirm an outside circumstance such as getting an approval from a governing authority, over a certain time period for the purchase or lease of the property.

OS&E

See Operating Supplies and Equipment.

Other Income

In real estate underwriting, Other Income refers to any revenue source not otherwise included in other income line items. Other income may include any number of revenue generators, from application fees to amenities fees. In the basic real estate pro forma setup, Other Income is combined with Total Rental Revenue to arrive at a Gross Potential Revenue line.

Owner Controlled Insurance Program

OCIP and CCIP are broad and all-encompassing insurance policies that usually cover, at a minimum, general liability insurance, worker's compensation, and excess liability insurance for all contractors and subcontractors on a construction project. An OCIP is sponsored and held by the owner, in contrast to a CCIP, which is sponsored and held by the contractor. The sponsor holds and is directly responsible for securing the appropriate and required insurance coverage.

Owner's Affidavit

A legal document signed by the seller of a particular property and provided to the buyer and title company that provides proof of ownership of said property. It provides factual information with regards to the legal status as it pertains to bankruptcy, liens, agreements, or judgments against the property.

Paid in arrears

See In arrears.

Pari Passu

A Latin term used to describe the equal treatment of investors, returns or securities. In real estate, the term is commonly used in waterfall distribution models to reference the pro-rata distribution of profits based on each investor's initial equity contribution percentage. The term is likewise commonly used to describe the cash flow from and to two or more lenders holding an equal position in the capital stack of a real estate investment.

Parking Income

In real estate underwriting, Parking Income refers to revenue derived from renting parking spaces at the property. In standard apartment, retail, office, and industrial underwriting, Parking Income is generally an Other Income item given that the income is secondary to the core rental revenue. In urban locations, however, where parking is scarce, the Parking Income earned may be substantial.

PCA

See Property Condition Report.

PCR

See Property Condition Report.

Permanent Financing

A long-term mortgage loan typically secured by a fully stabilized and performing real estate asset. A Permanent Loan (a.k.a. Permanent Financing) often includes a fixed interest rate with a longer loan term (7+ years). The permanent loan may or may not include an interest-only payment period for part or all of the loan term. These loans almost universally come with a penalty (e.g., yield maintenance, defeasance, % penalty, etc.) for prepaying the loan before maturity, and many include a lock-out period early in the loan term during which the borrower is forbidden from prepaying the loan.

Permanent Loan
See Permanent Financing.

Phase I ESA
See Environmental Site Assessment.

Phase II (ESA)
When the preliminary ESA exposes recognized environmental conditions (RECs), buyers will often require a Phase II ESA to provide a broader assessment of the property. A Phase II ESA includes a subsurface investigation, which tests soil, soil gas, and groundwater to reveal the source of any RECs. Of particular concern is the presence of petroleum products and other hazardous materials that may be on the site.

Power Retail Center
A power center is a retail subtype generally around 450,000 SF and larger, where you will find category-dominant anchors, including discount department stores, wholesale clubs, and off-price stores. Among their most common type of anchors are home improvement, discount department, warehouse club and off-price retailers. Power centers serve a trade area of 5 to 10 miles.

Source: ICSC

Preferred Return
A concept common to real estate partnership structures, preferred return refers to the preference given to a certain

class of equity partners when distributing available cash flow. The preferred return is generally calculated as either a percentage return on contributed capital or a given multiple on contributed capital and must first be paid before the sponsor / general partner has a right to promoted interest.

Premier Suburb

The most prolific, popular or expensive suburb within a city or town.

Prepayment Penalty

A fee charged by a lender for agreeing to allow a borrower to pay off a loan prior to the end of the contractual loan period. A prepayment penalty, or prepayment fee, is meant to cover the cost to the lender of a loan paid off prior to the agreed upon date, especially as it relates to the lender's reinvestment cost and interest rate risk.

Common forms of prepayment penalty in commercial real estate include a percentage of the outstanding loan balance, Defeasance, and Yield Maintenance.

Present Value

The lump-sum value today (time zero) of a string of future cash flows discounted back to today at a specified discount rate. In real estate, the Present Value of a real estate investment is the price that an investor would be willing to pay today for a string of future real estate cash flows to achieve a given target return (discount rate). In order to calculate Present Value, a discounted cash flow statement must be built forecasting the future net cash flows of a real estate investment.

Net Present Value is the Present Value of investment inflows (i.e., positive cash flows) less the present value of investment outflows (i.e., negative cash flows). In most cases, this means calculating the present value of all future cash flows and subtracting the amount paid for the investment in time zero.

So, if the Present Value of an investment is $1,000,000 and the investor must pay $750,000 to acquire that investment, the Net Present Value would equal $250,000 ($1,000,000 - $750,000).

In Excel, the Present Value is best calculated using the NPV() function, not including the value in time zero in the selected range. NPV is determined by calculating the Present Value then subtracting the amount invested in time zero.

Present Value Factor

Also called the Present Value of One or PV Factor, the Present Value Factor is a formula used to calculate the Present Value of 1 unit n number of periods into the future. The PV Factor is equal to $1 \div (1 + i)^n$ where i is the rate (e.g. interest rate or discount rate) and n is the number of periods.

So, for example, at a 12% discount rate, $1 USD received five years from now is equal to $1 \div (1 + 12\%)^5$ or $0.5674 USD today. The PV Factor can be used to calculate the Present

Value of a future stream of cash flows by multiplying each period's cash flow by the given PV Factor for that year and then summing the resulting values.

The PV Factor is the inverse of the related FV Factor or Future Value Factor.

Project Buyout

The Project Buyout is the time when the owner of a development project selects the General Contractor (GC) who then, either together with the project owner or alone, goes through the process of selecting and hiring all the subcontractors (subs) and pricing the project. A generic buyout process may look like the following:

Project owner selects the GC. The GC creates a list of subs for each trade and puts together Bid Packages or Requests for Proposals. These packages will include all relevant information about the project (drawings, specs, trade specific info., etc.), ask the subs to evaluate and respond with a price and all relevant information about themselves (proof of insurance, references, resumes, etc.). Based on the subs' responses and rate quotes, the GC will interview, select, and negotiate and sign a contract with the winning sub for each trade.

Promote

A financial interest provided to the sponsor (investment manager) as an incentive to maximize performance. This is typically an outsized share of the profits, payable once the investors have received back their entire initial capital contributions and achieved certain profit thresholds (i.e., preferred return). Promote is also referred to as the promoted interest or carried interest.

Promoted Interest
See Promote.

Property Condition Assessment
See Property Condition Report.

Property Condition Report
Also referred to as a Property Condition Assessment (PCA), the Property Condition Report (PCR) assesses the physical condition through a thorough inspection. It evaluates all of the improvements and various systems of each building on a property. Buyers or mortgage lenders may require items on the PCR be remedied before completing the transaction or funding loan proceeds.

PSA
See Purchase and Sale Agreement.

Purchase and Sale Agreement
A legally binding contract between a buyer and seller that outlines the terms and conditions of selling a property.

Quitclaim Deed

A Quitclaim Deed is a type of deed that transfers all interest the seller has or may have. However, there are no warranties of title and no guarantees against any encumbrances. This type of deed provides no legal recourse for the new owner.

Ratio Utility Billing System

A method of calculating a resident's utility bill based on specific factors such as occupancy rate or apartment square footage and then billing the tenant for their share of utility use. It is often used when the installation of sub meters is not financially feasible (due to the large up front capital investment) or economically feasible (due to a poorly designed utility configuration). The practice is becoming increasingly common as landlords seek ways to increase revenue and limit their cost inflation risk.

Real Estate Investment Trust

A real estate mutual fund allowed by income tax laws to avoid the corporate income tax. It allows investors, large and small, to participate in large real estate ventures without double taxation. A REIT sells shares of ownership and must invest in real estate or mortgage loans. Furthermore, a REIT must meet certain other requirements under the law: it must have a minimum number of shareholders, a widely dispersed ownership, and certain income tests. In the United States, a Real Estate Investment Trust must distribute 95% of its income to shareholders, which is not taxable at the corporate level but is taxable at the individual shareholder level.

REIT shares are either publicly or privately traded. Given that REITs are special entities tasked entirely (or almost entirely) with operating real estate, unique metrics have been created such as FFO and AFFO to help investors properly analyze the performance of these companies.

Real Estate Private Equity

Real Estate Private Equity, or REPE, is a term used to describe an individual or firm making direct investments in real estate using private capital, rather than public capital. This form of investment in real estate is generally thought of as high risk, high return given that the invested capital is most often the first *dollar* in, and the last *dollar* out. A firm that raises private capital to make direct investments in real estate is referred to as a real estate private equity firm.

Examples of large U.S. real estate private equity firms include Blackstone Group, Starwood Capital Group, and Carlyle Group.

Rear-load

Rear-load warehouses have the loading docks on the rear of the building, in relation to the street from which trucks enter. In other words, as a truck enters the property, it must drive to the rear of the building to access the loading docks.

Glossary of Terms A.CRE

Recourse

In real estate, *recourse* is the responsibility of the guarantor(s) of a mortgage loan to repay the loan in the event of borrower default. Similarly, a *recourse mortgage loan* is a loan in which the mortgage lender is protected against loss by one or more *guarantors*.

For example, the single-asset entity 555 Main St, LLC, acting as borrower, borrows from Mortgage Lender ABC $10 million to develop an apartment community. John Jones, acting as Principal Guarantor, personally guarantees the loan. In the event borrower defaults on the mortgage loan and should the foreclosure sale fail to satisfy the unpaid principal balance plus penalties, Mortgage Lender ABC has recourse to other assets owned by John Jones.

Regional Mall

These retail centers are connected by a common walkway, with parking generally surrounding the center's perimeter. Stores will include tenants with a full range of general merchandise, shopping services, and fashion offerings. Average regional mall sizes are over 500,000 SF, with a general trade area of 5 to 15 miles. Historically, anchors for this subtype have included full-line or junior department stores, mass merchants, discount department stores, and fashion apparel stores. However, this continues to evolve.

Source: ICSC

Reinforced Concrete

This refers to concrete in which wire mesh or steel bars are embedded into the concrete to increase its strength. In commercial real estate development and construction, reinforced concrete and steel framing add to the building's tensile strength, which allow for higher and more complex construction. Buildings with this construction generally cost more than comparable stick-frame buildings, and thus typically merit a higher valuation in comparison.

REIT

See Real Estate Investment Trust.

Renewal Option

A clause contained in a lease agreement giving the tenant the right to renew or extend their lease agreement. The option clause usually contains various predefined terms that both parties initially agree upon, such as a reversion to a market-related rental rate.

Rent Control

Rent Control includes laws that dictates the amount of rent a property owner/landlord can charge a tenant.

Rent Roll

The rent roll is a list of tenants in an income producing real estate asset and includes the property owner's reflection of all the rental income derived from the tenants at a specific time (usually at the end of the month). The rent roll often includes other information related to the tenants, such as a description of the space being rented, lease start/expiry dates and any security deposits held.

Rentable Area

Rentable area is the area within a building for which a landlord can charge rent. This includes the tenants' private and/or exclusive use spaces, as well as the building's common areas.

Tenants usually pay rent for their exclusive space plus a share of the common area. A tenant's rentable area calculation is commonly calculated by multiplying their usable space by the building's load factor.

Usable Area + Common Area = Rentable Area

REPE

See Real Estate Private Equity.

Replacement Cost

This is the cost to build a brand new, similar, and competing project in the same location as an existing building.

When underwriting a property, it is important to understand its value relative to the replacement cost. If a brand new and almost identical building can *feasibly* be built for cheaper on a per square foot basis in a nearby location than what it would cost to buy the project being evaluated, then the replacement cost is lower than the cost to purchase and the investor should consider passing on the property and/or developing the new project.

Residual Land Value Analysis

Residual land value analysis is a method for calculating the value of development land. This is done by subtracting from the total perceived value of a development, all costs associated with the development, including profit but excluding the cost of the land. The amount left over is the residual land value, or the amount the developer is able to pay for the land given the assumed value of the development, the assumed project costs, and the developer's desired profit.

Residual Pro Forma

Residual pro forma is the pro forma used to evaluate the residual/terminal value of a property. The residual pro forma seeks to forecast the net operating income a subsequent buyer might use in valuing the subject property. This figure often includes either the trailing twelve months (TTM) or the next twelve months from the sale date but can be altered to reflect a stabilized NOI at the time of sale.

Retention

Retention is a withholding of funds owed in order to increase the probability that the project will be fully completed to the standards initially promised by the contractor/subcontractor. An example of this would be an owner retaining 10% of the funds owed to the contractor

Glossary of Terms A.CRE

until the project is complete. This minimizes the risk of the contractor moving on to another job by ensuring incentives are well-aligned.

Revenue Per Available Room

Referred to in commercial real estate as RevPAR, Revenue Per Available Room is a metric used in hotel underwriting to calculate the amount of revenue each available room generates in a given period.

RevPAR is calculated by either 1) dividing the total actual revenue generated by the number of available rooms, or by 2) multiplying the hotel's average daily room rate (ADR) by the hotel's occupancy rate. The RevPAR differs from the ADR in that it accounts for any unoccupied rooms.

RevPAR = Total Actual Revenue ÷ Available Rooms

or

RevPAR = ADR x Occupancy Rate

RevPAR

See Revenue Per Available Room.

Right of First Refusal

Although they can be numerous in iterations, a Right of First Refusal, or ROFR (pronounced Rōfer), is a contractual clause that enables a third party to step in and purchase and/or lease a property based on what was negotiated between the Owner and a potential buyer/lessee.

As an example, let's say a tenant leases a building, and in that lease there is a ROFR clause to purchase the property if the owner decides to sell. In a more traditional ROFR scenario, if the Owner puts the building up for sale and negotiates with a potential buyer, upon coming to an agreement, the Owner would be legally obligated to take the negotiated terms and price to the tenant and offer the tenant the opportunity to step in and purchase the property first.

ROFR
See Right of First Refusal.

Rollover Loan
See Construction-Perm Loan.

RV Park or Resort
RV Parks consist of land organized into various lots or parcels for rent that accommodate recreational vehicles (RVs), either with or without services on the sites. Services typically include water, electric, and sewer. RV Parks can be set up to accommodate multiple types of end users, such as those using RVs for vacations to longer-term tenants using park model homes.

RUBS
See Ratio Utility Billing System.

Sale Leaseback

A transaction in commercial real estate where, upon completion of a sale, the seller immediately leases back the property from the new owner (i.e., buyer). The lease is generally NNN and long-term and converts the seller/lessee from an owner to a tenant. This type of transaction typically occurs where the business, financing, accounting, or tax benefits of leasing outweigh the benefits of owning. Some consider this mechanism a *hybrid* debt product, whereby the seller turned lessee decreases its actual debt load while freeing up capital.

Schematic Design

The first formal stage of the design phase after the conceptual design period, where initial design concepts are re-evaluated and many early-stage design documents are produced such as early iterations of site plans, floor plans, sections, and elevations. This phase is used to verify that the project is feasible and buildable and conforms to both the owner's and design team's vision.

Typical items studied during this phase are further function and form analyses, structural feasibility, MEP space layouts, vertical transportation, ingress, egress, generic exterior aesthetics, and floor layouts.

Seller's Title Affidavit

See Owner's Affidavit.

Short Sale
The sale of the property for less than the outstanding debt balance owed to all lienholders (typically senior and mezzanine debt providers). The property will fall into foreclosure if all parties do not reach a consensus agreement to sell.

Soft Costs
Any indirect development costs (i.e., not labor or materials). These costs range from architecture and engineering fees to project management and developer fees and can affect hard costs significantly (e.g., an architect's efficient building design may reduce the need for structured parking hard costs). Soft Costs are also referred to as Indirect Costs.

Sources and Uses
A schedule overview that details from where capital for a real estate project is sourced (sources) and how capital is deployed (uses). The *sources* side includes items such as loan proceeds and investor equity contributions, while the *uses* side includes items such as purchase price/construction costs and acquisition costs. Both sides must always balance.

Special Servicer
The designated party responsible for handling situations wherein the borrower defaults. A special servicer has

the authority to structure loan workouts or institute foreclosure proceedings. This is in contrast with a standard mortgage servicer who has limited legal power and is merely responsible for collecting rental payments from the borrower.

Special Warranty Deed

A special warranty deed will allow for recourse against the seller (grantor) if any issues (encumbrances or challenges to title) come after the transfer of the property to the buyer (grantee), which were created during the time that the seller owned the property. The special warranty deed will not protect the grantee against any issues or challenges to title that come up from the period prior to the seller's ownership.

Specific Performance

Specific performance is a legal concept that requires a party to abide by the terms of an agreement.

A simple example can be if a PSA is executed, and the seller subsequently decides not to sell the land. The buyer can sue for Specific Performance and a court can enforce the terms of the contract requiring the seller to sell based on the terms in the executed PSA.

Specifications Manual

A project manual that details the various products, construction materials and methods to be used in the project development.

Sponsor

The partner that "sponsors" a real estate investment. This individual or company is responsible for finding, acquiring and managing the investment. The sponsor generally brings market and property type expertise and plays the primary management role, while third party investors (limited partners) typically take on a more passive investment role. The Sponsor is also referred to as the General Partner (GP).

Springing Recourse

A form of loan guarantee only enforceable by a lender when certain default or credit events occur (e.g., if a borrower violates operating covenants, does not meet net worth requirements, files for voluntary bankruptcy, etc.). In springing recourse, or springing liability, when such adverse events occur, the borrower's guarantor (i.e., Principal) becomes partially or fully liable for loan obligations regardless of whether the loan is non-recourse or not.

Stabilization

Stabilization refers to a point in time when a property reaches its market potential in terms of occupancy, income, and expenses. This is commonly referenced in terms of Stabilized NOI, or the NOI once the property has reached that market potential.

In the case of value-add and opportunistic investments, stabilization occurs at some future point when the value-add or opportunistic strategy has been successfully executed. In the case of a core investment, the in-place NOI is assumed to be stabilized.

Stabilized Pro Forma

Stabilized Pro Forma refers to an income statement, wherein it is assumed that the projected income and expenses are underwritten at their market potential and are perpetual. One result of this analysis is the stabilized net operating income, which is an important input to direct cap valuation.

When building a stabilized pro forma, it is essential to assume that all income and expenses that go into the pro forma are stabilized (i.e. operating at market occupancy, rent, and expenses) and perpetual (i.e. the current state of income/expense will persist for the hold period and thereafter).

Stacking Plan

A visual representation of a building, similar to an elevation drawing, which shows the breakdown of space occupied by tenants on each individual floor. The breakdown may extend to include other details of the tenant such as their company name, occupied square footage, lease expiration date or rental rate.

Stick Framing

This simply refers to a construction method using wood materials for framing the structure. This method typically uses 2x4 or 2x6 dimensional lumber spaced 16" or 24" apart. Stick-built construction is generally allowed for structures up to five stories.

Stochastic Analysis

Also referred to as Probabilistic Analysis, Stochastic Analysis involves adding uncertainty to some or all of the inputs to the analysis such that the outcomes are likewise uncertain. In real estate financial modeling, this form of analysis allows the professional to better understand the range of outcomes (i.e. risk) possible in an investment.

The process of performing Stochastic Analysis first requires assigning probabilities to inputs and then simulating scenarios over and over again to capture the various outcomes that result from the uncertain inputs.

Stochastic Analysis is often paired with a technique known as the Monte Carlo method. This method involves repeatedly running simulations hundreds or thousands of times, recording the outcomes of each simulation, and then aggregating those outcomes to understand the mean (i.e., the expected outcome), standard deviation (i.e., the variation and range of outcomes), minimum value, and maximum value of all of the outcomes.

Storage Income

In real estate underwriting, Storage Income refers to income derived from renting storage space to tenants. In apartment, office, retail, and industrial underwriting,

Storage Income is generally an Other Income item given that the storage space is typically leased to existing tenants at the property.

Strip or Convenience Center

This retail subtype is characterized by having a row of stores, with on-site parking often found in the front of the stores. Open canopies may be used to connect store fronts of the tenants at the center. Average size may be 10,000 - 15,000 SF and larger, with a trade area of less than 1 mile. A typical anchor for these types of centers may be convenience stores, such as a mini mart.

Source: ICSC

Structured Parking

Any above-grade or below-grade, ramp-accessible structure capable of accommodating vehicle parking. A multi-level design allows for greater parking densities and increasing land use efficiency.

Structural Engineer

Structural engineers are a type of civil engineer. A key task of the structural engineer includes determining and analyzing the forces of each element in a structure. The engineer must ensure that all of the structural elements of a building have the ability to counteract all the loads that may impact it.

Subcontractor

A company that specializes in a specific component of a project and is hired by the General Contractor and/or ownership to work on a development project. Some examples of subcontractors are plumbing, electrical, HVAC, drywall, glazing, insulation, and masonry.

Super-Regional Mall

This retail subtype has a higher variety and assortment of tenants than regional malls. They have an average trade area of 5 to 25 miles and average over 1,000,000 SF in size. Typical anchor types reflect the same as found in regional malls.

Source: ICSC

Survey

A survey confirms crucial information about the location and existence of a property through boundary lines and a legal description. It will include information about physical improvements on the property, such as utility, parking, and building information, as well as details on access, property setbacks, encroachments, easements, or any other zoning violations that affect the property. Surveys will also indicate whether a property sits in a flood plain or other hazardous area. Common survey types include the following: as-built, boundary, and ALTA (American Land Title Association). An ALTA survey is the industry standard for most due diligence requirements.

Tax Increment Financing

A financing method used by government to incentivize urban renewal and development within targeted areas. When new development occurs in the TIF zone, the property's incremental taxes (above a fixed baseline amount) will be allocated to a TIF fund. These funds are then allocated towards infrastructure improvement and job creation within the TIF district, which in turn leads to higher property values and further private investment.

Takeout Loan

A type of permanent financing used to repay the proceeds owed on existing short-term debt (e.g., a construction loan). Takeout loans are typically structured with longer terms, fixed payments and other structures commonly seen in permanent mortgage loans.

Temporary Certificate of Occupancy

A certificate of occupancy issued prior to project completion allowing the tenant or owner occupancy of a space while construction is still ongoing. A Temporary Certificate of Occupancy, or TCO, typically expires within a finite time period, which varies by jurisdiction and property type.

Tenancy by the Entirety

A type of property ownership unique only to married couples. In all other forms of ownership, when there is more than one owner, each owner has a part ownership in the property. With tenancy by the entirety, each spouse owns the entirety of the property.

Tenant

See Lessee.

Tenant Estoppel Certificate

A document signed between a landlord and a tenant verifying certain facts are correct (such as whether or not a tenant is in good financial standing with the landlord). Tenant Estoppel Certificates are often required by lenders when financing a property or by a prospective buyer as part of their due diligence.

Tenant Health Ratio

See Occupancy Cost Percentage.

Tenant Improvements

A form of inducement typically seen in office, retail, and industrial real estate; tenant improvements (TIs) are physical changes to a tenant's leased space to accommodate the specific needs of the tenant. TIs may include building or moving interior walls or partitions, floor covering, shelves, windows, doors, bathrooms, etc. The cost and who bears responsibility for the work is a negotiation between the tenant and the landlord. TIs are generally quoted as an amount per square foot (or per square meter). They are most often offered at the beginning of a newly signed, or newly renewing lease.

Tenant Rollover Risk

The risk associated with expiring lease agreements at a property. This risk includes the possibility of not being able to re-lease the space should a tenant vacate or, alternatively, the possibility of signing a lease but on less favorable terms than the previous lease.

Tenants in Common (TIC)

An ownership structure whereby two or more individuals may own an equal or unequal, undivided share in a property. This partnership structure enables lower income investors the opportunity to purchase more expensive real estate, which they otherwise may not have been able to afford individually. However, when mortgaging a property, the lender will also require that all co-tenants share joint liability for the loan, thereby increasing the risk of a TIC structure.

Theme Retail Center

Theme- and festival- retail centers generally have entertainment as a unifying theme. You will find tourist, retail, leisure, and service-oriented offerings. These centers are generally located in urban areas, or as part of mixed-use projects. Restaurants and entertainment options are common anchor tenants for this retail subtype. The centers serve a much larger trader area of 25 to 75 miles and average around 150,000 SF and larger in size.

Source: ICSC

TIC
See Tenants in Common.

TIF
See Tax Increment Financing.

TI's
See Tenant Improvements.

Time Value of Money
The idea that money received today is worth more than the identical amount of money received in the future. This is because money received today can earn interest over time as well as increasing costs of goods and services over time due to inflation, thus making a dollar more valuable today than in the future. The time value of money is a core principle of finance and the foundation of various return and valuation metrics used in real estate (e.g., PV and IRR).

For example: $100 received today, when grown by 2% per annum, becomes $110.41 in five years. Thus, $100 received in five years is worth less than $100 received today.

Title
A document that lists the legal owner of real property, and which must be transferred in a sale of the property. The title will reflect the form of ownership, which may be a sole ownership, joint tenancy, tenancy in common, or others.

Title Affidavit
See Owner's Affidavit.

Title Insurance
A form of insurance that protects property owners and/or lenders against any property loss arising due to legal defects on the property being transferred (outstanding liens, encumbrances on the property etc.).

Title Search
A real estate title search will examine any public records available in an effort to confirm the legal owner, as well as to determine if there are any liens or claims on the property by other parties, such as property tax liens or mechanics liens.

Title Theory States
Title theory states are those states in which the borrower in a loan on the property does not hold the property's title during the loan term. Rather than a mortgage, the lender holds the title through a Deed of Trust. Once the loan is paid off, the lender, through a Deed of Reconveyance, removes its interest in the property and transfers title back to the borrower.

Total RevPAR
Where RevPAR divides total revenue *from room sales* by available rooms in a given period, Total Revenue Per Available Room (TRevPAR or Total RevPAR) is a metric

that includes total revenue *from all hotel departments in addition to room revenue*. Other departments are typically and formally categorized as F&B, Other Operated Departments, and Miscellaneous Income.

Trailing Twelve Months

A Training Twelve Months (TTM) value is a reflection of a property's last 12 months of financial performance. The TTM report shows actual historical data rather than forward looking estimates (typically presented by the broker) in the OM, thereby helping the investor make a more informed valuation of the property.

Transfer Tax

A charge levied by a state or local government when property is sold from one individual or entity to another.

Trended Rents

Rental rate figures which are based upon some market growth projection. Trended rents use historical market data as an indicator of future growth, in contrast to "untrended rents" which assume no growth in annual rents.

Real estate discounted cash flow models, which account for rental growth, generally are capable of calculating the trended rental rate of an investment at some future date.

TRevPAR

See Total RevPAR.

Trophy Asset

A term used in real estate to describe a property that is in exceptionally high demand by investors. These assets are usually iconic buildings situated in prime locations with strong underlying property fundamentals.

Trustee

When debt is placed on a property, a trustee is a third-party entity that holds legal title to the property until the borrower fully repays the loan. Requirements to be a trustee vary by state. Whereas a trustee must be authorized by certain law to serve in that position in some states, others have no limitations on who or what entities may serve as a trustee. Common entities that serve as trustees in real estate lending scenarios include title companies, banks, credit unions, and attorneys.

TTM

See Trailing Twelve Months.

UCC Foreclosure

Related to UCC Article 9, this type of foreclosure generally occurs when there is mezzanine debt encumbering the property. When a mezzanine borrower breaches any term or is in default, the mezzanine lender has the option to foreclose on the borrower's collateral interest, which is an interest in the entity that owns the real property rather than on the real property itself. This type of foreclosure is a faster and less expensive process than a foreclosure on real estate would be. *See also Mezzanine Debt.*

Under Water

A situation wherein the outstanding loan balance exceeds the open market value of the property. This limits the owner from selling the asset and, unless a loan workout is negotiated, the property will be foreclosed.

Unlevered Cash Flow

The net cash inflows and outflows of a real estate investment before taking into account cash flows related to financing. Unlevered cash flows generally consist of total investment costs, net operating cash flows before financing, and asset reversion cash flows (i.e., net proceeds from sale). In real estate financial analysis, the unlevered cash flow line is used to calculate the unlevered internal rate of return and unlevered equity multiple of a prospective real estate investment.

Urban Infill

Repurposing property in an urban environment for new development. The term implies that the surrounding area is mostly built up and what is being developed will "fill in" the gaps. Urban infill usually focuses on repositioning underutilized buildings and is often part of a community redevelopment program.

Usable Area

Space in a project that is available exclusively to the tenant for use. This is usually office or retail space over which the tenant has sole control.

Building common areas are not included in usable square footage.

Valet Trash

A trash collection service, most common in multifamily properties, offered by the landlord to remove trash from residents' doorsteps and deposit the waste into the dumpster or compactor area. Residents are typically charged for the service and in many cases the service is mandatory.

Value Add

A real estate investment strategy categorized by medium-risk and medium returns. A Value-Add strategy typically involves acquiring under-performing assets with upside potential and adding value through one or more repositioning strategies. These strategies may include property renovation, tenant realignment, operational improvements and re-tenanting strategies, among others, with the goal of boosting net operating income, thus increasing the value of the property.

Variable Costs

Costs that vary based upon of the property's level of

operation and performance. For example, property management fees vary directly based on the property's revenue and therefore will likely be higher with greater occupancy of the building. This is in contrast to Fixed Costs, which do not vary with the property's level of operation and performance.

Variable Rate Debt
See Floating Rate Debt.

Vertical Expansion Option
A real option which allows the owner of a development project to build and complete the project to a certain height with an option to increase the height of the building at some future point. The cost of a project when building with this option is estimated to add a 5-10% premium on standard construction costs due to implementing building systems and components that may be excessive for the current building size. However, this expense may be offset by the risk reduction benefits associated with the increased development timing flexibility and potential cost savings in the future phase of development for having built a majority of the building in a previous period.

WAL
See Average Life.

WALE
Abbreviation for Weighted Average Lease Expiry. *See*

Weighted Average Lease Term for definition.

Walk Score

A score assigned to a property which measures and allocates a value from 0 - 100 based on the property's ease of access to public transport and other nearby amenities.

Walkability

A measure of how amenable an area or property is to walking. The most popular measure of walkability is the "Walk Score," which measures and allocates a score to a subject property from 0 - 100 based on its ease of access to public transport and other nearby amenities.

Wall Street Journal Prime Rate

The Wall Street Journal Prime Rate is the interest rate charged among the largest banks in the United States. The rate is not linked to the federal funds rate, although there is typically a 300 basis points (3%) spread between them. The WSJP rate is widely utilized by lenders as an index against which other loans are measured, e.g., WSJP + 1.5%.

War Room

In real estate, the "War Room" is generally a virtual depository of vital investment-related information necessary to perform due diligence on a deal. Practically speaking, the "War Room" is a collection of computer folders, shared with stakeholders to a deal, which contain financial information, property reports, maps, statements, and other investment-specific information necessary to transact a real estate investment.

Warehouse

Warehouses are generally one-story buildings with high ceilings that typically have multiple dock high doors that can accommodate large trucks for loading and unloading inventory. Warehouses may have a small amount of square footage dedicated as an office component for support staff, with the larger proportion dedicated to storage and distribution.

Warm Shell

Any building/rentable area that has been minimally fitted out with basic services (such as ceilings, lighting, plumbing and HVAC) and is ready to lease to the tenant. Usually these "warm shell improvements" -- necessary to convert the building from a cold shell to a warm shell -- are only completed following signature of the lease agreement in order to alleviate the Landlord paying for unnecessary improvements that the Tenant may not require. The transition from a "Cold Shell" to a "Warm Shell" is referred to as the "Build-out."

WAULT

Abbreviation for Weighted Average Unexpired Lease Term. *See Weighted Average Lease Term for definition.*

Weighted Average Lease Term

A metric in commercial real estate that measures how much contract rent is remaining at the property. Specifically, the WALT measures the weighted average remaining contract lease term for all tenants at a property. Generally rental income is used as the weight in calculating the weighted average. Weighted Average Lease Term is an important measurement for analyzing office, retail, and industrial properties.

The term is synonymous with WAULT (weighted average unexpired lease term) and WALE (weighted average lease expiry).

To calculate the weighted average lease term:

1. Multiply the current rent by the remaining lease term for each of the tenants.
2. Sum the total of results from step 1.
3. Divide the result from step 2 by the sum of current rent for each of the tenants.

Weighted Average Life

See Average Life.

Wrap Up Insurance

An insurance policy for larger construction projects that typically covers general liability insurance, worker's compensation and excess liability coverage over the entire construction period for all contractors and subcontractors involved in the project. There are two types of wrap up insurance, namely Owner Controlled Insurance Program (OCIP) and Contractor Controlled Insurance Program (CCIP).

Yield Maintenance

A method for calculating prepayment penalty, yield maintenance considers the difference between prevailing interest rates and the contractual interest rate of the loan such that the borrower does not benefit from changes in interest rates, and the lender is not disadvantaged by changing interest rates.

Yield Maintenance is generally calculated by finding the present value of the remaining cash flows due to the lender, discounted back at an agreed upon discount rate using an agreed upon benchmark rate (e.g. government bond yield), less the outstanding loan balance at the time of prepayment.

Yield-on-Cost

Yield-on-cost, also known as development yield, is the net operating income (or sometimes cash flow from operations) at stabilization divided by the total project cost, whereas the capitalization rate (cap rate) is the stabilized net operating income (or sometimes cash flow from operations) divided by the market value of the property.

Yield-on-Cost = Net Operating Income at Stabilization ÷ Project Cost

The yield-on-cost serves to help the real estate investor calculate the difference between the market yield and the actual yield of an investment. In development, this difference between market yield (market cap rate) and actual yield (yield-on-cost) is called the development spread.

Zero Cash Flow Property

A real estate investment where all excess cash flow from a property goes to pay down the senior mortgage. Zero cash flow investments are generally leased to credit-rated, single-tenant NNN tenants due to their highly secure/safe risk profile, and the loan is sized and crafted such that the debt service equals the lease payments and the loan term and amortization match the lease term.

Much of the benefit of owning this type of property comes in the losses, due to depreciation, over the hold period that offset gains on other investments in an investor's portfolio. Modeling the taxable losses is essential to understanding the yield of such an investment.

Notes

Glossary of Terms

A.CRE Glossary of Terms

Glossary of Terms

Want to learn
REAL ESTATE FINANCIAL MODELING
in just weeks, and without all the guesswork?

- MODEL YOUR OWN DEALS
- LAND THE JOBS
- GET AN EARLY PROMOTION

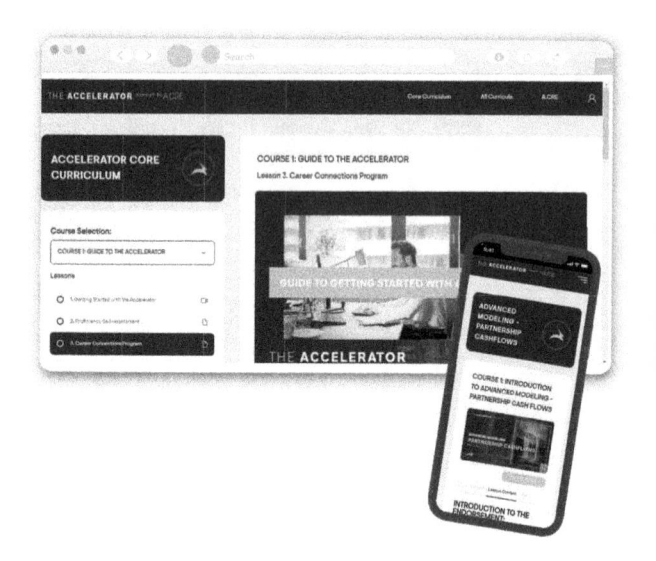

Scan the QR code below to learn about
the A.CRE Accelerator.